Relic

Land/Water and the Visual Arts

EDITED BY LIZ WELLS AND SIMON STANDING

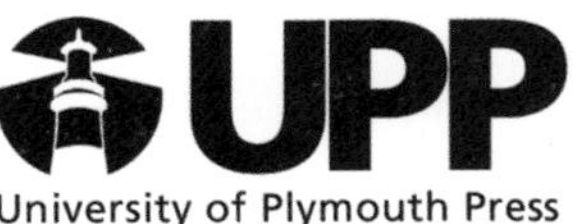

University of Plymouth Press

© 2009 University of Plymouth Press
A catalogue record of this book is available from the British Library

ISBN 978-1-84102-223-9
Library of Congress Cataloging in Publication

Publisher: Paul Honeywill
Book design: Yulia Razina
Cover image: Guy Moreton

Address: Liz Wells, Scott Building, University of Plymouth,
Drake Circus, Plymouth, Devon, PL4 8AA

CONTENTS

INTRODUCTION

To say that European landscapes are sprinkled with legacies and reminders of past cultures and events is to state the obvious. Histories are marked in the present, through stories told and through marks on the landscape, relics of former activities and events. Layers of history testify to the over-laying of one era on another; motorways run on routes established by the Roman legions; standing stones inter-relate pre-historic cultures and the business modes of contemporary heritage industries.

This is the fourth in a series of publications based upon the annual summer symposium run by Land/Water and the Visual Arts. The theme for 2007 was 'landscape and relic'. Six speakers approached 'relic' from diverse positions that variously invited us to consider the biographic, the microscopic, specific moments in art history or grand narratives, as well as critically reflecting upon their research processes as artists, on medium and method.

Ian Walker's focus is upon Swanage, the South coast town where Paul Nash and Eileen Agar lived briefly in the mid-1930s. His account at one level represents his personal quest to note surrealist effects of various architectural legacies of a period in the nineteenth century when an exchange of Purbeck Stone and London artefacts introduced a number of 'displaced' items to the town, where they remain, present in Nash's imagery traced through Walker's re-photography. Objects (benches; a clock) remain in use and thus have contemporary currency whilst simultaneously – if we pause for a second glance – reminding of an earlier uneasy disassociation.

Tim Edgar likewise explores a layering of history on the South coast, specifically a cave on the Dorset coast, a legacy of former quarrying. The focus is more specific; in certain respects it reads as an example or case study through which desire to investigate and understand the sedimentation of culture over historical time can be illustrated. But, remnants of human activity – cigarette stubs testifying to a beach party, perhaps – inter-twine with natural sedimentation as stones and leaves erode or decompose forming transient surface patterns. As a photographer, the challenge is one of indicating fluidity using the photography which, as a medium, has been associated with static moments. Resolution within 'grids' which simultaneously contain and order a number of images whilst allowing for distinctions between discrete moments pictured is explored as a response to the photographer's conundrum, namely, how to represent fluidity and change through stillness.

Artist-film-maker, Zineb Sedira, tackles a similar methodological conundrum, namely, the problem of presenting parallel narratives through film, an essentially linear medium, which she uses in conjunction with photography. She explores the post-colonial complexity of

Algerian culture, with its French and Arabic influences, as symbolised particularly through the comings and goings in the port area. In common with the work of many diasporic artists, the sea here symbolises fluidity and cultural crossover, operating literally as geo-political boundary and metaphorically in terms of complexities of subjective identity. Perhaps paradoxically, in terms of choice of medium, much of her endeavour in concerned to combat semblances of representation and fixity often associated with lens-based media. But on second glance, this paradox is part of the point: 'unfixing', implying histories marked not only on architectural facades but also beneath the surface, pointing to inter-secting histories and biographies, is conceptually and aesthetically integral to her project.

Harriet Tarlo walks. For her the physicality of the encounter with particular places is central to her response to place. As a poet her notebook is central; but ideas are made manifest not only through language, but also through performance or through the typographic rhythm of the page. For Tarlo, as for many other contemporary writers, meaning is enhanced through affects of material textures – words as staccato markings within performance or affectual shapes within the page, echoing John Cage's emphasis of the significance of silence.

Questions of language and meaning have pre-occupied twentieth century philosophy, particularly analytic philosophers such as Wittgenstein who moved both from Austria to Cambridge, and from a quest to understand language in terms of logistics to the proposition that meaning and communication are effects of experiential context and the social usage of words. He did not specifically address the visual arts, but artists frequently reference both his search for contemplative places to work and, in terms of the content of his musings, his insistence that verbal language can do no more than indicate – or point to – meaning which is, as he demonstrates, fluid.

Wittgenstein's house on the West Coast of Norway (Skjolden, Sognefjord, north of Bergen) has become something of an icon of intellectual refuge – places for reflection, and, by extension, for thinking through making. Guy Moreton acknowledges Wittgenstein's repeated returns to the house overlooking the fjord when noting his own wanderings in East Anglia. This interest generated a trip to Norway to experience for himself the peace of the woods by the fjord, from which emerged a body of work on Wittgenstein's – and, by extension, our own – desire for reflective solitude. For Moreton, Wittgenstein's mode of philosophical investigation becomes a springboard for reflections on spaces of creativity; being in, experiencing and moving through particular landscapes energises awareness.

Jeremy Diggle directly draws on Wittgenstein's theoretical musings, demonstrating, through performance, the evocative nature of words. Unlike Moreton, Diggle never made it to Skjolden, but a piece of wood, designated by colleagues as a relic of Wittgenstein's outhouse, acts as a starting point for an imagined pilgrimage; he conjures up a sense of place through describing (ostensive) images of the location and remains of a dwelling which he himself never saw and which he assumes his audience has not visited. Wittgenstein's insistence that meaning does not reside innately in words, or even in grammar, but rather emerges through processes of use and interpretation, is evoked. We don't believe the speaker, but we cannot avoid becoming embroiled in speculation, each creating our own unique vision or idealised rural refuge.

Together then, the papers testify to the diversity of ways in which 'relic' may be interpreted as a concept, the extent to which histories are embedded in the everyday and may be over-looked or act as imagistic triggers for speculations about space, place, past and present. They also indicate a range of problems tackled by artists seeking the means to express something of a response to remnants from the past and ways in which medium and method, conceptually and intuitively, themselves contribute to articulating particular complexities from the past as marked in the present, and through their re-marking, becoming a past moving into the future.

Liz Wells and Simon Standing
May 2009

Ian Walker

Seaside surrealism:
a visit to Swanage

In 1935, Paul Nash wrote an essay entitled 'Seaside Surrealism', in which he described the town of Swanage - where he was living at the time - as a sort of Surrealist 'terrain vague', where urban disquiet invaded the natural landscape. He was particularly fascinated by the various monuments that inhabited the town. These had been brought there in the nineteenth century by John Mowlem and George Burt, the owners of the local quarries. Whenever they shipped a boatload of Purbeck stone to London, the ships would return with items from the city - a clock tower from Westminster Bridge, a Wren façade from one of the guild halls.

This text traces Nash's itinerary through Swanage, examining how, in such a setting, subjective fantasy can interweave with objective reality.

It is with a sense of mounting anticipation that we head south across the heathland, and, as we catch the first glimpse of the afternoon sun on the sea, start the descent down the hill to Swanage Bay. On the sea front, we stop, walk to the edge of the esplanade where the sea is lapping up on the beach and take in the geography of the bay.

It faces east and is framed by the twin headlands of Ballard Point to the north – the white cliffs glistening in the last of the sunlight – and the much lower Peveril Point to the south, which sits on the other side of the pier. But it's not just the pleasures of sea, sun and sand that make this a moment to remember. I'm afraid that I am not here on a childhood holiday, excitedly clutching my bucket and spade – rather this visit to Swanage is the culmination of several years serious and rather adult research. Still, I must admit that I'm awfully excited to be here.

I've been to Dorset several times previously but never to this end of the county. I've walked along the Cobb at Lyme Regis, scrunched through the pebbles on Chesil Beach and photographed in the deserted, lunar quarries on the Isle of Portland. But I've never made it to Swanage, even though I've increasingly known that I need to come here, in order to give a reality to all the images of the place I've been looking at and all the things I've read about it.

What has recently centred my interest on Swanage is the research I've been doing into the time that the artist Paul Nash spent here between Autumn 1934 and January 1936. A study of this period when Nash painted, photographed and wrote about the town is going to form a chapter in a book I've been working on, looking at the conjunction between Surrealism, photography and concepts of Englishness. The work that Nash made in a number of sites - the megalithic rock circle at Avebury, the shattered trees in Monster Field as well as here in Dorset - is one of my starting points, and I've been spending a considerable amount of time digging in archives and libraries.

Most of these have been in London. The Hyman Kreitman Research

Centre is a low, dark, temperature controlled space in the basement of the Tate Britain, where I've worked my way through the Nash archive – all his photographs as well as boxes of letters, postcards, notes and catalogues. In another basement, under the Courtauld Institute, I looked through old copies of the *Architectural Review*, which in April 1936 published the pivotal essay that Nash wrote on 'Swanage or Seaside Surrealism'. Higher up, in the airy spaces of the National Art Library at the Victoria and Albert Museum, I have pored over an original copy of the *Shell Guide to Dorset*, which Nash worked on while he was living here. And, in the calming pastel reading rooms of the British Library, I've called up guidebooks to provide a plethora of background information – books with titles like *Swanage Past and Present, The Swanage Encyclopedic Guide, Swanage and Purbeck: Photographic Memories* and *The Sixpenny Guide to Swanage*.

Already, then, as in Nash's own work, there is a tension here between Swanage and London, between the site of origination and the site of preservation and display, between city and country, between the hard pavements and the sandy beach. (Sous les pavés, les plages, indeed!) The fact that some of the most significant buildings in London are built with Dorset stone adds a very tangible edge to this relationship - if you look closely at the walls of St. Paul's Cathedral, you'll see Dorset fossils embedded in them.

So, to resolve all this, I have to go to Swanage itself. Hence this journey and my excitement at finally standing here. But I also know that my visit cannot be innocent – I cannot now, suddenly, let the wind off the sea blow out of my brain all the information and images I've accumulated over the past couple of years. I know that I must inevitably experience Swanage through the photos I've been looking at and the history I've been reading. Such a lack of innocence is, of course, a little saddening and part of me wishes I were here just to play with my bucket and spade. But nevertheless, it's possible to revel in the tainted but intriguing fact of being in this place with all this stuff in my head and letting the two collide. And I know that the process will also reverse itself – that not only will I experience Swanage through its photos, but that the photos will also be changed by the experience of Swanage. The simulacrum hasn't won yet – nor I think will it, as long as there is a wind blowing off the sea.

Perhaps, while the light fades and before I explore Swanage in earnest tomorrow morning, I should explain why Paul Nash found it so 'surrealist' and why in consequence I am here. Traditionally, Swanage's main trade was the quarrying and shipping of the local Purbeck stone. In the mid-nineteenth century, this trade was dominated by John Mowlem, who founded the construction firm that still bears his name today. He particularly developed the trade with London and, to ballast the ships on the way back, he would collect fragments of demolished monuments and street furniture from the capital, with which he then embellished Swanage.

His nephew George Burt took over the business after Mowlem's death in 1868 and was even more ambitious. Thomas Hardy dubbed him the 'King of Swanage' and he built several other extraordinary local monuments using fragments from London (as well as developing the town's growing reputation as a respectable seaside resort). But, of course, what Mowlem and Burt thought they were doing is not the same as how it has subsequently been viewed. In retelling their story in 1936, Paul Nash dubbed them 'those eminent mid-Victorian surrealists'; if the title is justified, it demonstrates rather well that the best surrealist effects are often achieved by those who don't know they are surrealists.

The next morning is bright and sunny, though there are threats of rain later. First off we drive a little out of town, south to Durlston Head, where George Burt built his grandest sequence of monuments. High on the headland is the mock gothic Durlston castle, while below it a complex of paths wind down to the old abandoned quarry workings at Tilly Whim Caves. All along the way Burt had carved a mixture of pious exhortations and factual commentary. On one rock at Tilly Whim, it says 'LOOK ROUND AND READ GREAT NATURE'S OPEN BOOK'.

The site is dominated by the Great Globe, a representation of the Earth carved in Purbeck stone, weighing 40 tons and measuring 10 foot across. Nash called it the 'largest of the jokes' but in fact, it has a presence that is far more substantial than that. It is indeed a strange presence to find here looking out across the Channel, but it is also a very impressive work of sculpture. Its substance and its strangeness come together to memorable effect – I photograph it obsessively while knowing that no photo can convey the sensation of placing my hand on its haunch and feeling its weight and texture.

That's a wonderful start. Coming back into town, I head out on foot, working my way down the High Street from the old church of St Mary's, which was at the centre of medieval Swanage. Nash referred rather caustically to 'a few old stone houses still standing at the time of going to press'; they're still there, though rather done up now. Just down the hill, one comes to Purbeck House, the mansion that George Burt built for himself in a style that Nikolaus Pevsner dubbed 'High Victorian at its most rebarbative'. It's a hotel now and one can, with permission, wander its gardens at leisure. These are lavishly but rather randomly decorated with salvage material from a variety of London buildings – balustrades from Billingsgate, columns from Waterloo Bridge, an arch from Hyde Park corner and statues from the Royal Exchange. Next to the entrance, there's a cast of the Parthenon Frieze.

Over the road from Purbeck House is the Town Hall, originally a rather plain building transformed in 1881 by the addition of a façade which had originally been on Mercers' Hall on Cheapside in the City of London. Burt and Nash after him thought it had been designed by Sir Christopher Wren in 1670; now it seems more likely it was by his pupil Edward Jerman. Still, it's not the sort of façade one expects to come across in a quiet seaside town - a Baroque confection of garlands and drapery with a couple of cute cherubs above the main entrance.

At the bottom of the High Street is the sea. I sit for a while on the seafront esplanade just along from where Paul and Margaret Nash lived at no. 2, the Parade, eating a bag of chips that I'd bought from no. 1: the Parade Fish Bar. The salt on the chips seems to merge in my throat with the salt in the air off the sea and, here and now, this seems like the most natural food one could imagine. I watch the holidaymakers on the seafront, determined to make the most of this autumnal warm spell, and, for a few minutes, I forget about Nash, Mowlem and Burt as the present fills my nostrils.

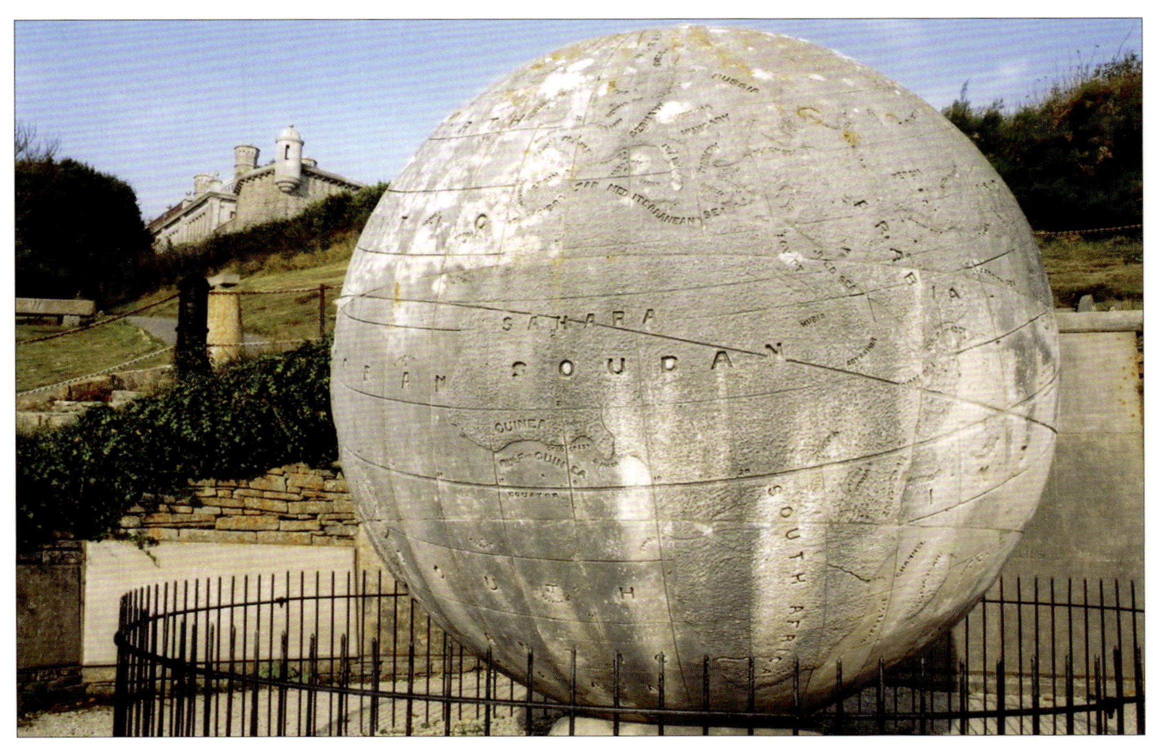

The Great Globe

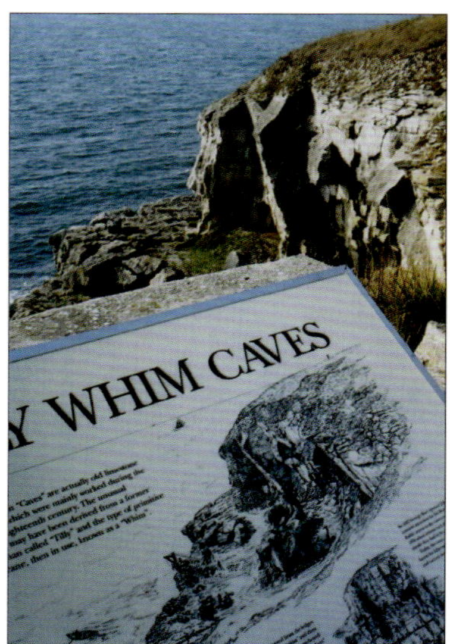

Tilly Whim caves

Along the esplanade is the Mowlem Theatre, a modernist box built in the 1960s to replace the Mowlem Institute, which Nash had called 'the most dismal building in Dorset'. The theatre isn't much better but, next to it, stands a monument built by John Mowlem himself – a stone column surmounted by a pyramid of cannon-balls. Looking round for some historical event to commemorate, Mowlem hit on the (alleged) defeat of the Danish fleet in Swanage Bay by the ships of Alfred the Great some thousand years before in 877 AD. The actual cannon-balls used on the monument were, however, Russian and had lodged themselves in the hull of a British ship during the Crimean War. Some have wondered about the appropriateness of these missiles to commemorate a sea battle fought 400 years before the invention of gunpowder.

As one wanders from monument to monument, one comes across less formal and official objects which take their meaning and their resonance from their setting here in Swanage. Nash himself liked the new seats placed along the seafront, in which as elsewhere he fancifully saw the symbolic form of the swan. Their white concrete supports punched through with a rhythmic pattern of holes made him think perhaps of the sculptures of his friends Henry Moore or Barbara Hepworth and he dubbed the seats 'Swanage modernism'. Today, alas, they have gone from the seafront, but we did find one, looking the worse for wear, tucked away behind the old railway station. It should, I think, be restored.

But not all such discoveries have their source in Nash's observations. One of my own favourite moments today was when I was up at Purbeck House and I saw that the metal columns surrounding one part of the

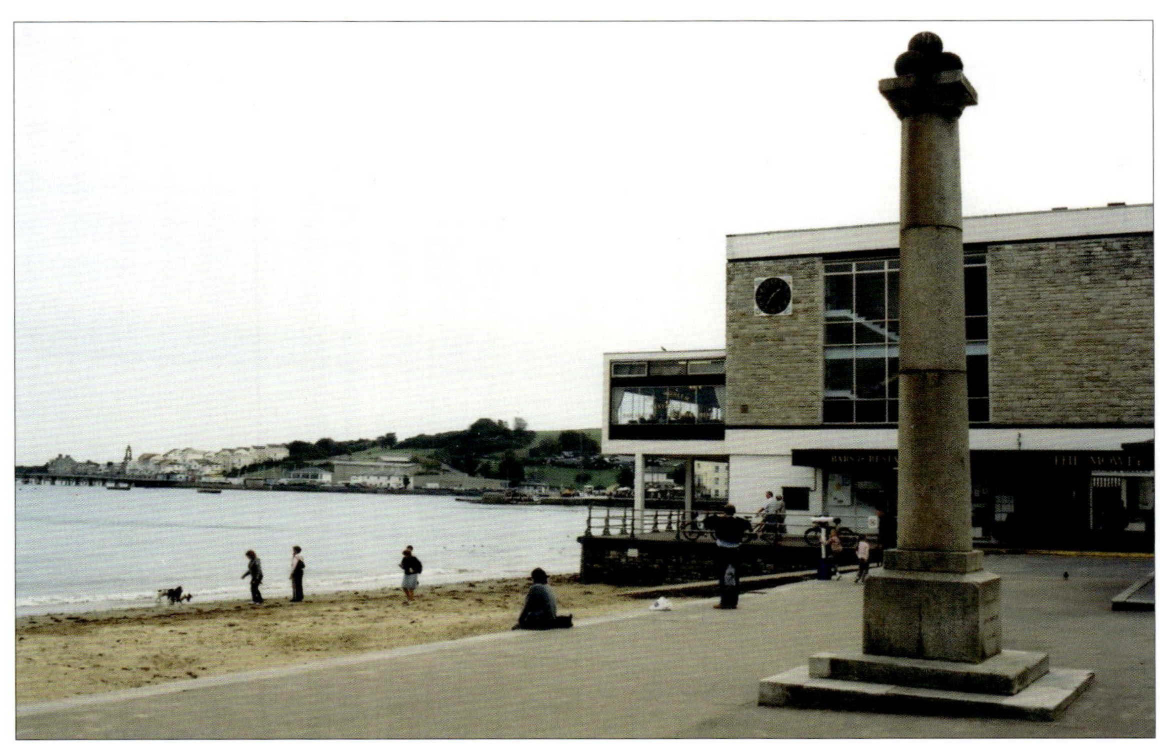

Alfred the Great Column

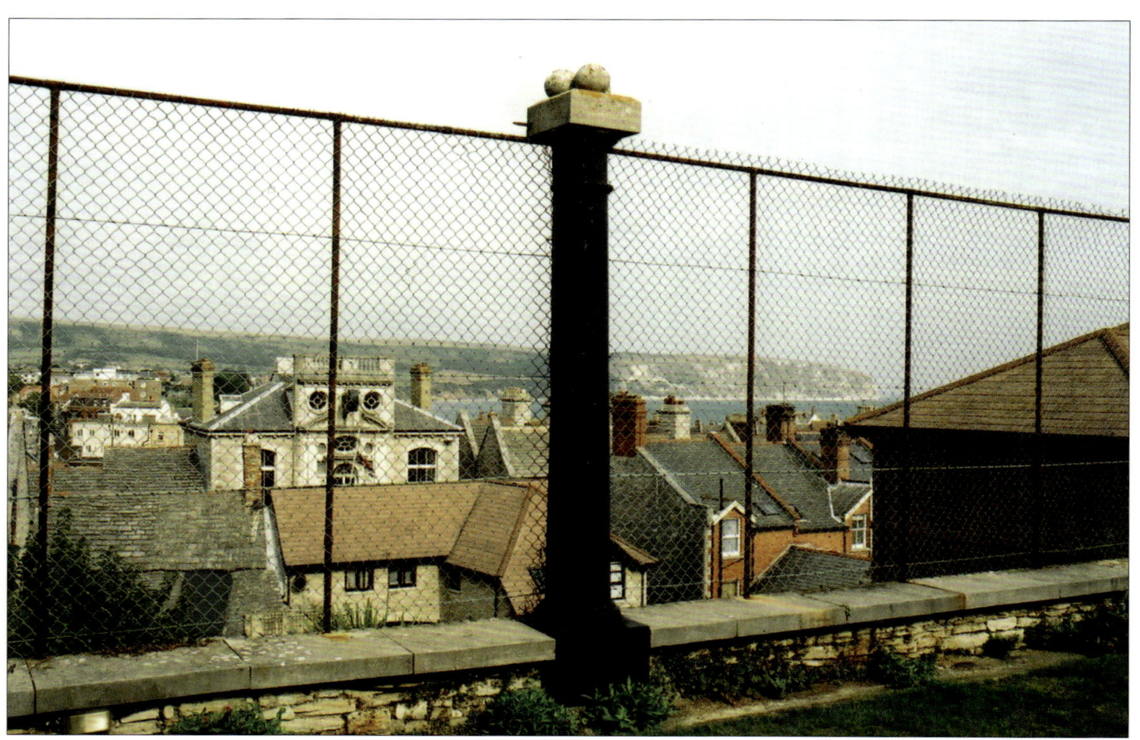

Tennis court at Purbeck House

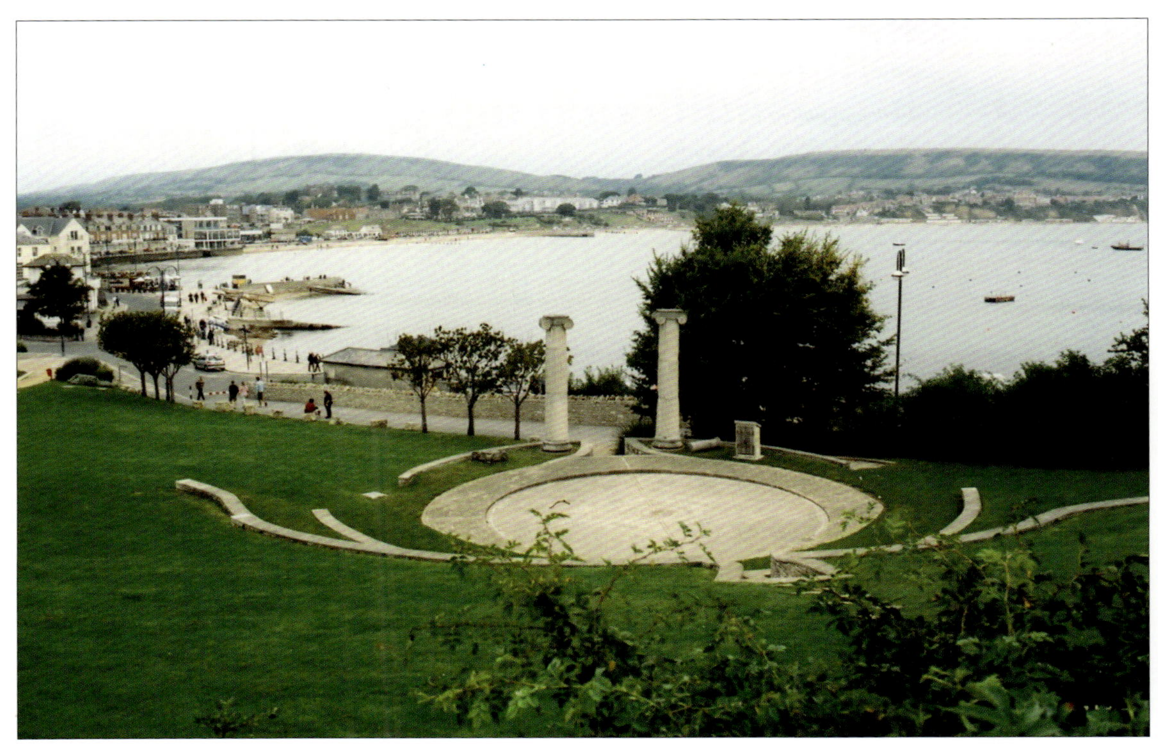

Grosvenor Columns

garden mimicked the Alfred the Great monument. And, with a note of delight, I realised that this part of the garden had actually been the tennis court and the spheres on top of these columns were intended to be not cannon-balls but tennis balls, alternating with (somewhere exhausted looking) metal rackets.

The sky is clouding over now and I hurry on along the seafront to the final sites I want to see. Around the bay towards Peveril Point is the pier and next to that, in a patch of greensward that sweeps down the hill, are placed a couple of Corinthian columns. This is the site of the Grosvenor Hotel, demolished in 1986 but, in Nash's day, one of the grandest of Swanage's buildings. The columns originally stood at its entrance – now they have lost even that function.

And finally, out on Peveril Point, there is the gothic clock tower, which, as Nash noted, is clockless. Built in 1854 as a memorial to the Duke of Wellington, it had originally stood at the southern end of London Bridge. But it got in the way of traffic and so, in 1866, it was brought to Swanage and sited here on this headland, where it majestically – if a little pointlessly – looks out across the bay. Nash photographed it set against the white cliffs of Ballard Head in the distance and seemingly rising from the undergrowth in the foreground. (The undergrowth has now, perhaps inevitably, been replaced by a parking lot for pleasure boats.)

I walk along the water's edge and out on the Pier, but the rain is settling in now and I spend more time looking at the photos of old Swanage in the little home-made museum than standing outside, breathing in the sea air. Walking back through the drizzle, along the seafront and up the High Street, I watch the holidaymakers packing

Wellington Memorial

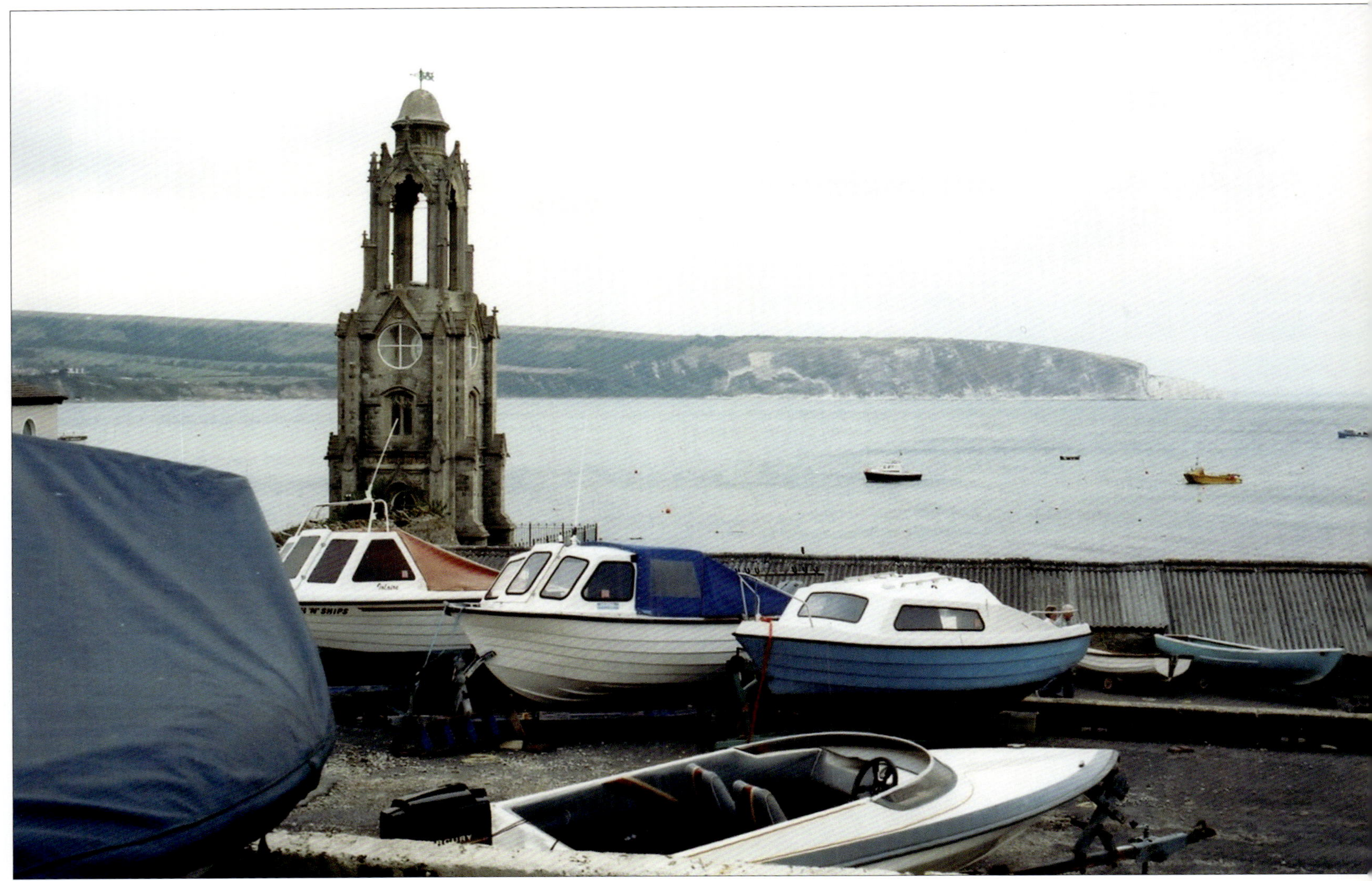

up and heading out, their brightly patterned leisurewear now hidden under anoraks and plastic raincoats. In defiance, I buy an ice-cream cone and sit in a shelter thinking about this day.

It does feel a little strange when I'm undertaking one of these explorations, as if I'm in a bubble, moving through a different space, almost a different time zone, from everyone around me. Nowhere in this town can I find any reference to Paul Nash's time here - not even a blue plaque on his house. And how many of the people walking round the town today - residents or visitors - know or even wonder what these monuments mean and how they got to be here? Of course, it's arrogant to assume that you are the only person to whom something like this matters, or, indeed, to think that these layers of knowledge are in themselves more valuable or precious than whatever else is in the heads of all these other people. But you do, in this situation, suddenly become very aware that you simply don't know what the people around you know, what their emotions are, why they are here and what this place means to them.

Each of us carries in our head a freight of assumptions that are partly communal - how else would I know that chips and ice-cream are the right things to eat here? - and partly very private. And the ideas and associations we bring with us merge inextricably with the things we find when we get here. Whatever that mix of assumptions and associations might be for any individual, I find it hard to imagine an altogether innocent vision - rather a range of visions informed by a plenitude of experiences.

For myself, I know about Mowlem and Burt and Nash and I can't escape that knowledge. But neither do I want to. Somewhere near Swanage, Paul Nash once photographed a block of steps, standing alone and isolated on a hillside. As I'm walking along the seashore from the Wellington monument to the Pier, I see another set of steps which end abruptly in the seawall. No doubt they once had a purpose, but right now I love their pointlessless, their lack of functionally turning them, as it were, into sculpture. Of course, I see them the way I do because I've seen the photograph that Paul Nash made of his steps and I enjoy that connection. It seems to me an enrichment of my experience of this place, rather than a confinement.

The next morning is sunny again. Before I leave, I drive down to the seafront. The tide is higher now and it splashes lazily up on to the pavement. I lean on the railing in front of no. 2, the Parade, and look out across the bay. There are moments like this when one wishes time would stop, the experience would freeze and be held for ever. But it doesn't. I look at my watch, go back to the car and drive up the hill, away from the sea and towards this desk where I'll sit to recollect the experience. Though I know - thankfully - that its essence must remain elusive.

Now, it's three years later and my book was published several months ago. Maybe now it's out there, making its own way in the world, I can go back to Swanage, walk down the path to Tilly Whim and simply enjoy it for its own sake. Maybe.

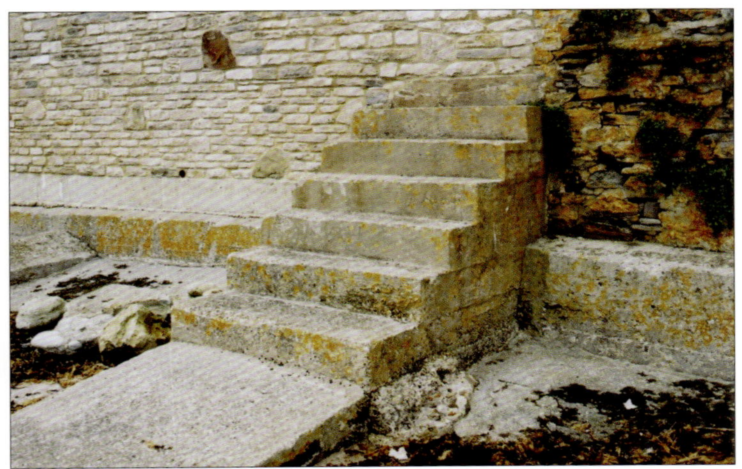

Steps on seawall

NOTES

For a thorough account of Nash's time in Swanage, see Pennie Denton, *Seaside Surrealism: Paul Nash in Swanage* (Swanage: Peveril Press, 2002). It also contains Nash's essay, *Swanage or Seaside Surrealism*, first published in the *Architectural Review*, April 1936.

The most detailed study of the work of Mowlem and Burt is David Lewer and J. Bernard Calkin, *Curiosities of Swanage, or Old London by the Sea* (Swanage: Purbeck Press, 1999). There are extensive details of Burt's two major building schemes in David Lambert's essay, *Durlston Park and Purbeck House: the Public and Private Realms of George Burt, King of Swanage*, New Arcadian Journal, 45/46 (1998), pages 15-52.

I want to extend my warm thanks to Tim Edgar and Kate McGrail for their hospitality in Swanage.

So Exotic, Some Homemade: Surrealism, Englishness and Documentary Photography is published by Manchester University Press, 2007; see Chapter Three, *Seaside Surrealism: Nash at Swanage*, pp. 32-51.

Tim Edgar

Subterrane: remnants from a cave

As an introduction to Edgar's practice, there is an overview of previous work, in particular, Rookery. This touches upon the broad theme of nature / culture and how locations with defined boundaries are generally chosen as sites, and is followed by a look at the current project Subterrane which draws upon photographic conventions from Archaeology and Space Exploration. It is inspired by the surface of a cave system formed by quarrying at Winspit on the Dorset coast. Historical and contemporary marks and remnants are used to examine relationships between place and time. Emphasis is on the process, in terms of recording and classification and editing and cataloguing. In conclusion the paper focuses on meanings realised through the conjuncture of remnants past and present, and the positioning of the work in relation to the conventions it references.

I first came across the caves at Winspit, on the Dorset coast near Worth Matravers, on a Sunday afternoon walk with my family. The expansive cave system that remains is the result of quarrying for Purbeck Stone, which stopped in 1945. On a bright afternoon, entering the caves, my

fig 1 *(Untitled, from Subterrane 2007)*

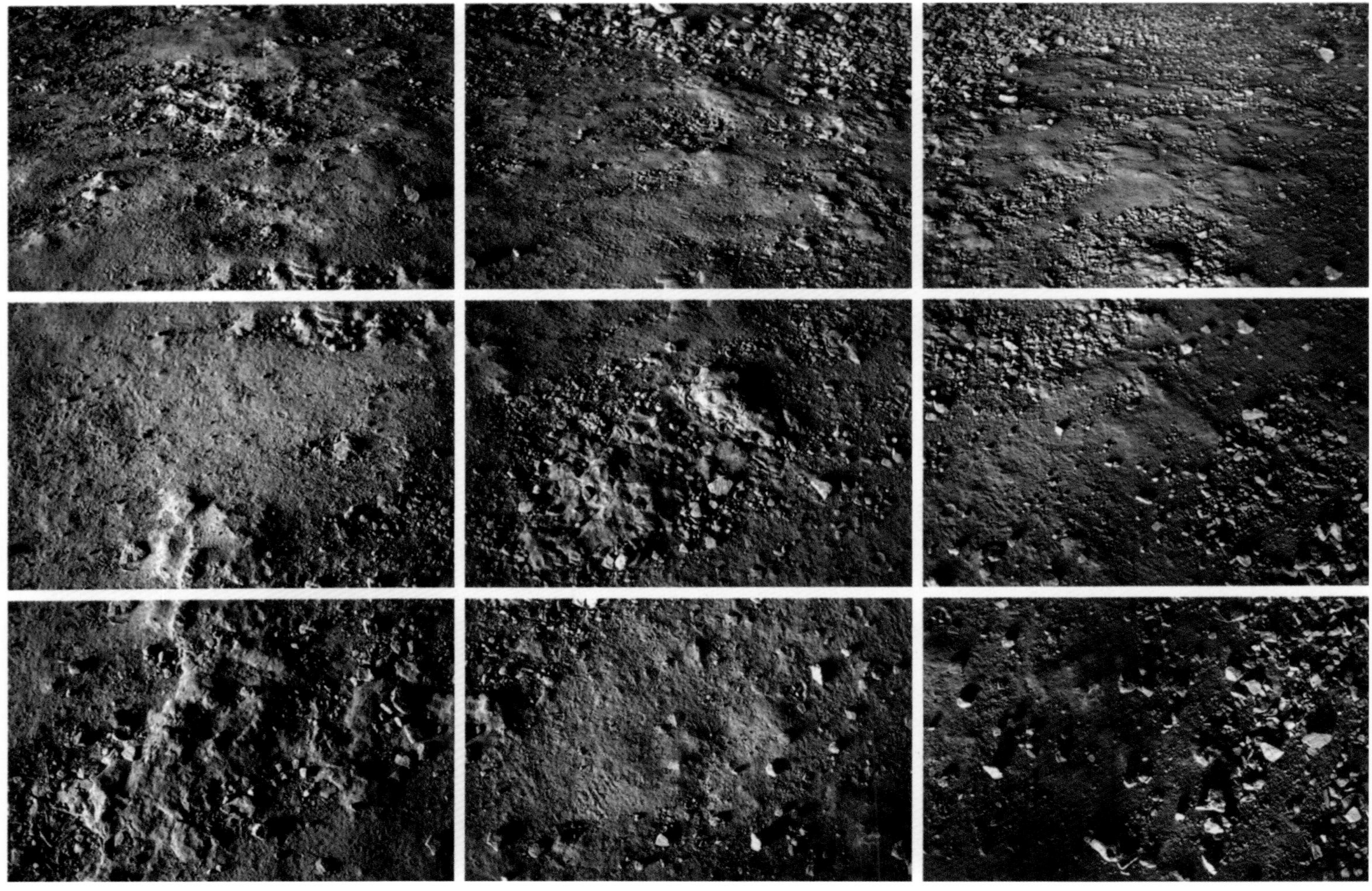

eyes took a while to adjust to the dark interior. I was struck by the ground, the colour and detail of the surface and the light's quality and direction. These formal qualities gave it the appearance of a planetary surface, spatially disorientating.

With black and white film in my 35mm camera I instinctively attempted to record the surface. With no tripod, the camera's aperture at F2.8, the shutter at 1/15th of a second, and my meter indicating around 2 stops underexposure, I was confident only of some sort of basic record of the scene. My lens was unable to take in the whole scene, so I took 3 photographs scanning progressively further into the cave, moved to my right and repeated the scan, and then to the right again for the final 3 images. A week later I collected the 9 enprints from the processors expecting little. On piecing them together I was surprised by the outcome, being transported back to that Sunday afternoon and that first powerful impression (fig 1).

That first impression has stayed with me and continues to inform my visual strategy in producing a body of work that I have since titled *Subterrane*. Even now, 5 years on, entering the cave and the process of visual adjustment allows me to enter another world.

Christopher Tilley in his extensive writings on the Phenomenology of Landscape suggests that:

> Spatial knowledge requires the coupling of an accumulated time of memory to overcome an initially hostile and alienating encounter with a new place.[1]

That first encounter of mine was alienating and unsettling. I was for a moment unsure of time and place. I have since made many visits, exploring the caves surface and contents, trying to piece together the evidence as some sort of forensic archaeologist. This on-going exploration is, though, not an attempt to overcome that initial "alienation", that is still key to my aesthetic response and something I wish to hold on to.

The grid has become a key formal visual strategy to help me represent the complex phenomenological aspects of the cave experience. This method of representing "space" is familiar from the records of space exploration. That first construction (fig 1) revealed a complexity far removed from the immediate snapshot practicalities of its making. The slight "overlap" between the sections I initially viewed as problematic, and considered technical approaches to ensure accurate connection. On further reflection I felt, and still do, that this added a certain quality, successfully representing the experience of scanning a large surface area and its spatial conundrums.

A detail revealed on inspection, surprisingly not noticed at the time of taking, was the footprint in the foreground. This clearly influences the works reading in several ways. It references further the iconic images from Apollo missions, acknowledges human presence, especially that of me the Photographer, and gives the viewer the opportunity to attempt to configure the scale.

On revisiting Rosalind Krauss's chapter "Grids" in *The Originality of the Avant-Garde and Other Modernist Myths* I found, to no great surprise, that her thoughts have considerable relevance to my use of the grid in this context. Setting out the grid as a key component of modernist practice, particularly important to the Cubists, and a major tool in their quest for a new way of interpreting 3 dimensions, she further suggests that the grid:

… is what art looks like when it turns its back on nature[2]

Drawing upon the modernist practice of Mondrian and others, a tension is set up between the content of the cave grids, which is fundamentally nature in its primitive state, and the lines of the grid. The randomness of the cave floor's surface is exaggerated by the constraints of the grid. Space and time are expressed differently through landscape detail and graphical strategy.

Mark Rothko used the grid and its constraints less rigidly. The majority of his paintings use the vertical grid as a base for sumptuous experimentation with colour relationships. However concrete references to the grid lines are abandoned and there are less defined grid edges. Colour and space merge, boundaries between the sacred and the everyday are undefined, representing the Artist's own spiritual position.

On the grid's relationship with the interpretation of space Krauss observes that:

Logically speaking, the grid extends, in all directions, to infinity. By virtue of the grid, the given work of art is presented as a mere fragment, a tiny piece arbitrarily cropped from an infinitely larger fabric[3]

Unlike the single photograph, Krauss implies that the grid actually suggests further images to the viewer, beyond its boundaries. For the cave floor then, the grid helps to signify an infinite surface.

However Krauss' most important points relate to the grid's relationship to higher matters, and to the representation of the relic.

The grids mythic power is that it makes us able to think we are dealing with materialism (or sometimes science, or logic) while at the same time it provides us with a release into belief (or illusion or fiction)[4]

She uses the key painting by Ad Reinhardt, *Abstract No 9*, 1966 to illustrate her key point:

… we could think about Ad Reinhardt who, despite his repeated insistence that "Art is art", ended up by painting a series of nine black square grids in which the motif that inescapably emerges is a Greek cross. There is no painter in the West who can be unaware of the symbolic power of the cruciform shape…[5]

In *Subterrane*, the relics, as stones or found remnants, refer to both historical and contemporary activity, objects both of use and of spiritual attachment, a dichotomy that is rich territory for the grids own conflicts. The grid seems then through Krauss' definition, an appropriate vehicle for exploring the relics position in this context.

Another grid work (fig 2) shows a central crater with ashen fallout

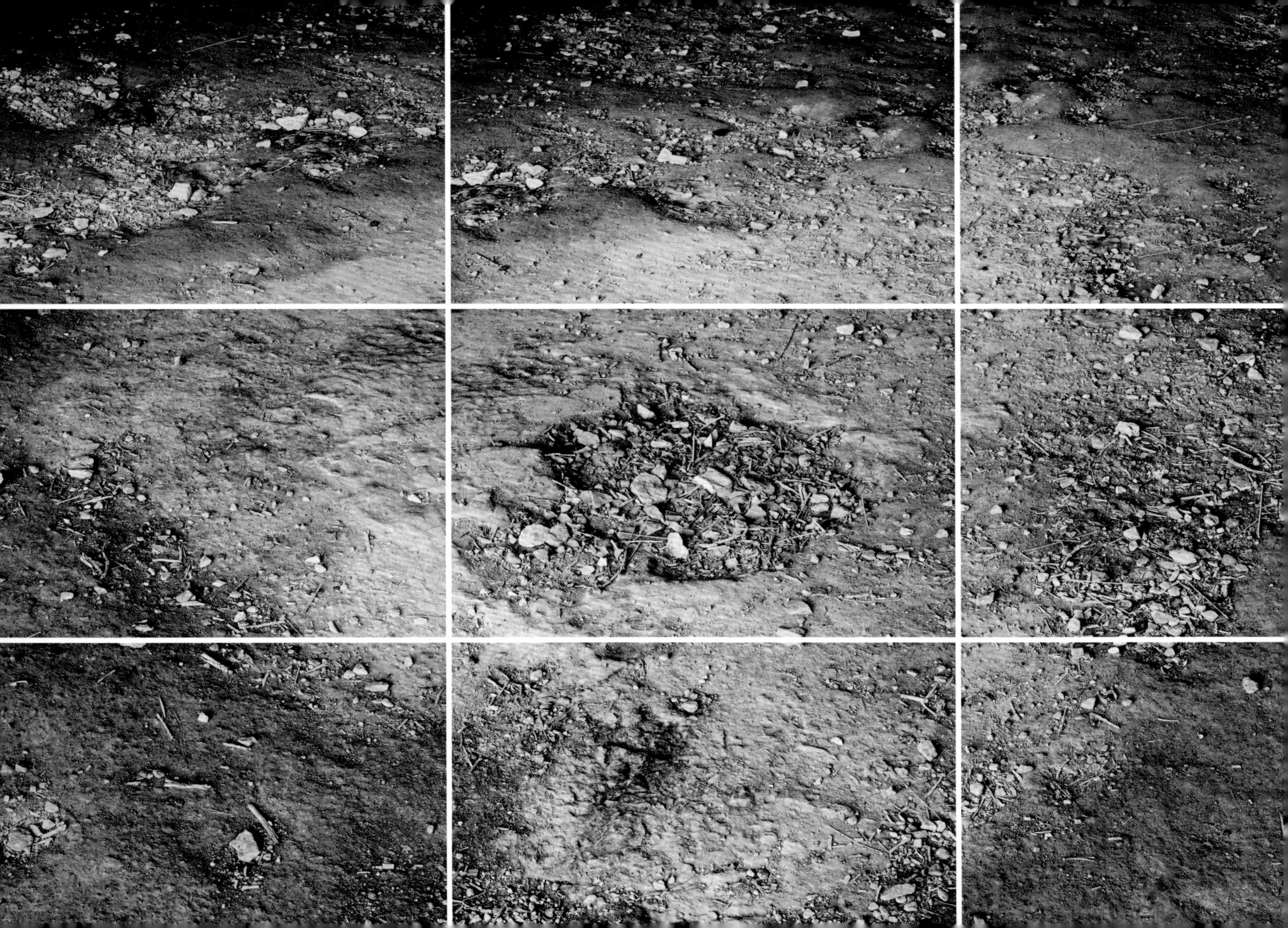

fig 2 *(Untitled, from Subterrane 2007)*

fig 3 *(Untitled, from Subterrane 2007)*

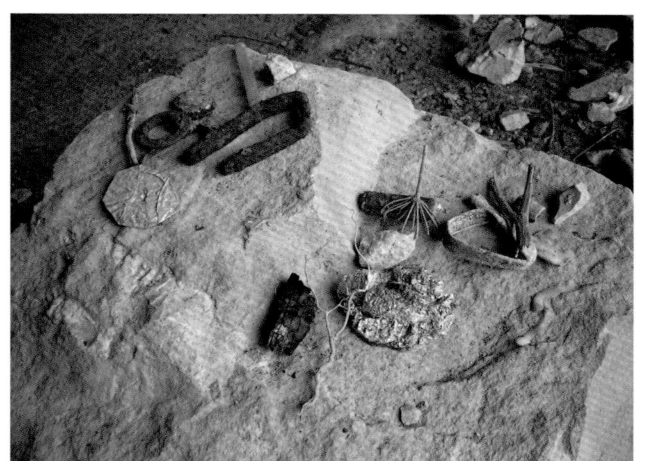

fig 4

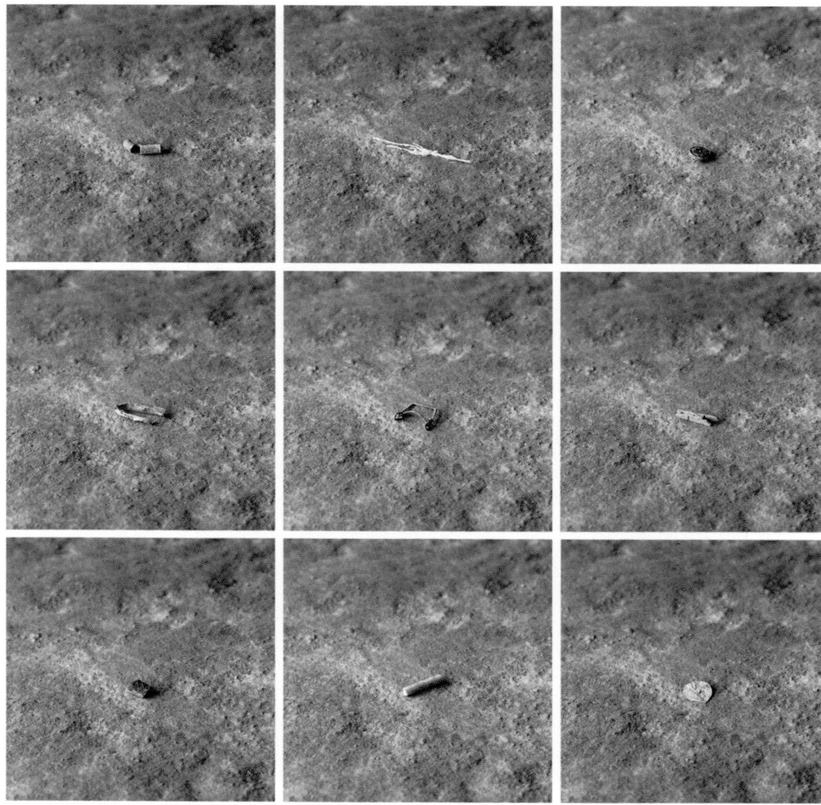

fig 5
*(Untitled, from
Subterrane 2007)*

spreading towards the edges of the image. The cross like construction of the 9 image grid is emphasised by the organic nature of the ground's pattern on the cave floor. This central crater is significant as it can be read in a number of ways; the remains of ceremony, trace of meteorite, or volcano crater. Most readings return to a "primitive" one reinforced by the presence of the cross through the 9 section grid.

Although the grid of 9 remains my primary strategy, I have also experimented with the grid of 3. The triptych, a well known device of painters from history, was the standard format for alter paintings from the middle ages onwards, and continues *Subterrane's* relationship with the sacred.

Using a ground level viewpoint (fig 3), the darkness above the curved horizon suggests infinity, implies vastness and confuses reading of scale, again employing visual conventions borrowed from the recording of space exploration. The foreground stones although miniscule, appear monumental. The shallow depth of field further accentuates this reading of the image as an infinite primitive landscape, one for exploration and recording.

The discovery, within the complex surface detail of the grids, of remnants of human activity (often left from Parties in the cave) led to new photographic strategies for me, including the investigation of Archaeological Photography and its conventions.

On some visits to the caves I would focus, with the aid of a torch, on the collection of objects of interest. These were collected on a large stone "table" (fig 4) and then photographed as a studio Photographer might photograph a commercial object, against an appropriate background, using a medium format camera and tripod. In an attempt at "objectivity" the camera was never moved and the background remained the same, allowing the found "evidence" to speak.

Like all areas of photographic practice, Archaeological Photography has its own problematic conventions. The use of a camera on a kite, balloon or even small aeroplane to record aerial views of a site is commonplace. Here we have similarities with reconnaissance photography and again with the photography of planets. At times as with the cave constructions these aerial surveys are disorientating. Such issues of calibration when photographing objects of archaeological interest are overcome through the use of a "Photographic scale". Lighting should be flat, objects should fill the frame, everything should be in focus, and backgrounds should not affect the reading of the object.

Sudeshna Guha's writings on the nature of Archaeological Photography and its role in the creation of histories, reveal some of the complexities in this area:

…. the historiography of archaeological representations alerts us to the epistemic shifts through which "evidence" gets constituted differently at different points of time, and the instrumentality of the representations within these shifts breaks all possibilities of according them with "fixed" meanings[6]

Looking at another grid work (fig 5), this time constructed differently, being made up of single object images taken in the "cave studio", we

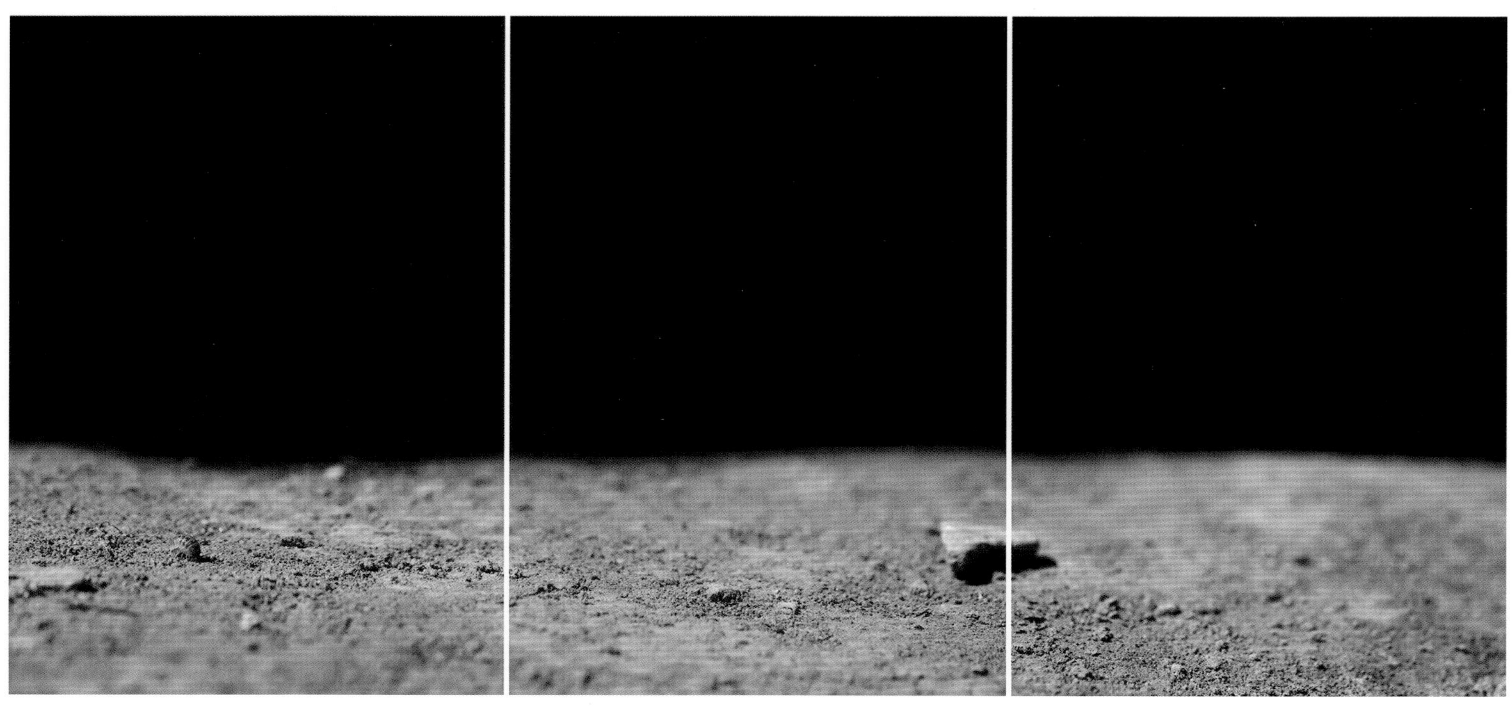

fig 6
*(Untitled, from
Subterrane 2008)*

32 Tim Edgar

can see how the use of some of the conventions referred to above, contribute to a variety of possible interpretations. The size of the objects is easy to establish due to the presence of some which are easily identifiable such as the peg and battery. Lighting is even and they are in focus so detail is represented.

Problems arise though when attempting to make literal sense of the grid. The objects do not fill the frame, robbing them of significance in relation to the dominant background that becomes central to any interpretation. The background is "timeless" and signifies the primitive landscape. As Guha has pointed out (see above), it is impossible though to give this evidence a fixed meaning. A title and a date would clearly help, however the objects themselves affect each other's representation leading to a problematic narrative. Due to the use of conventions relating to archaeological practice where objects are assumed significant because they are singled out for photography, the viewer wrongly assumes here that these objects are significant. A reading is attached to it that comes more from the viewer's history and experience than it does from any intentions I may have had as the Photographer. The viewer automatically attempts to piece together a "story" which is made difficult because some of the objects are difficult to identify, disrupting the narrative.

A clearer narrative though is established in the most recent work (fig 6), which draws together some of the primary contextual references. The focus has shifted to "survivors" in the cave, in particular the elusive Woodlice, timeless creatures from prehistory, as they explore the surface of their barren "planet". These creatures represent hope amongst the ash and dust, helping to position the work more clearly in the context of the exploratory space missions trying to find new life in our solar system.

My intention with *Subterrane* is to represent the caves activities and histories through the collection of its remnants past and present, and encourage subjective "narration" through the use of some of the questionable conventions of objective "documentary" representation. This approach compliments some of the key concerns of the "grids", and the project as a whole, those of historical, spatial, and temporal disorientation and questioning.

NOTES

[1] Christopher Tilley (1994), *A Phenomenology of Landscape: Places, Paths and Monuments*, Berg Publishers, p. 28.

[2] Rosalind Krauss (1985), *The Originality of the Avant-Garde and Other Modernist Myths*, The Massachusetts Institute of Technology Press, p 9.

[3] Ibid, p 18.

[4] Ibid, p 12.

[5] Ibid, p 10.

[6] Sudeshna Guha (2006) *Archaeological Photography and the Creation of Histories in Colonial India*
www.harappa.com/photo-archaeology/introduction.html

HARRIET TARLO

Love/Land: writing outside
in the twenty-first century

In this essay, Tarlo introduces her site-specific poetic practice around land and water within the context of concerns with landscape, environmentalism and representation. She locates her open form writing within the context of Charles Olson's poetics. She outlines her research into the particular suitability of experimental or "linguistically innovative" techniques, such as open form and the use of the unstable subject, to an environmentally-sensitive perception of landscape. The essay includes extracts from Tarlo's poetry, focusing in particular on works written over a period of many months of walking through specific, local places. The human being's place in the locality and the landscape is not erased, but is questioned. Tarlo asks how we might draw on, rather than deny, our desire for the landscape around us without encapsulating the non-human solely within our own frames of reference.

"The act of trying to say is always an act of location" (Charles Olson)

In considering land and relic, my modernist/experimental inheritance, my interest in landscape and environment and the significance of locality to my poetry are all pertinent. In particular, I want to focus on work around land and water, my most significant experience of which is the Cornish coast around Padstow, a place I have visited since before I was born. It is also worth mentioning that there is a strong Northern influence in my work as I lived in Northeast England for the best part of ten years and have been in West Yorkshire now for twelve years. The talk/reading was something of a retrospective exercise for me in which I revisited and updated a piece I wrote about "writing outside" for an anthology which came out in 1990 as well as looking back over my work for representative selections.[1] In this essay I reprint a few of the poems I read, but do not of course have space to print the full reading.

For me, the emphasis on poetics, on form over theme, that is found in experimental or linguistically innovative poetry does not marginalise or eliminate the material world, but strengthens the stimulating tension of work which engages with the "outside" in new ways. In my critical work I have identified various experimental poets who are working on rural and semi-rural areas and coined the term "radical landscape poetry" to differentiate their writing from traditional lyric nature poetry. The poets Colin Simms, Maggie O'Sullivan and Frances Presley are among some important contemporary influences, in particular for their dynamic use of sound and of space on the page. Like these writers, I write in the open form tradition historically associated with the American poets of the Black Mountain group and usually seen as originating with Charles Olson's *"Projective Verse" manifesto* (1950). *"Projective Verse"* has inherited many followers on both sides of the Atlantic and beyond, as contemporary poets will readily testify. Kathleen Fraser', has talked about the "immense permission-giving moment of Charles Olson's *"PROJECTIVE VERSE" manifesto*" and Jack Foley's recent essay, *"Projective Verse at 50"* argues that its influence goes way beyond those poets who consciously acknowledge it.[2] Olson advocated "kinetics": the energy of sound and movement embodied in open forms. Words are not restricted by set margins, left hand justification or stanza form, but are instead spaced more freely on the page in order to invoke and embody the sound, rhythm and energy of speech. Although I have some reservations about Olsonian rhetoric, I use his work as a springboard here because, for me, his innovative ideas about form and about the human being in his/her environment broke significant ground and are still relevant today. Olson's other name for open form writing was "composition by field", a phrase that the poet Robert Duncan extended. His notion of the open form poem as a field is also crucial to many contemporary open form poets who are interested in landscape.[3] In my critical work about "radical landscape poetry", I have argued, some would say contentiously, that:

"...the more dynamic, open form style of writing, which makes use of the whole page-space to create, is particularly suited to reflecting on and engaging with the spatial. For me, this has indeed been the openness of a cliff or seascape, field, moorland, or hillside, those spaces in which we see human and non-human elements at work as on a canvas in the open air. Here, poets might even attempt to embody the vast, complex, inter-related network of vegetation, insect and animal life that such a space contains, and to reflect intelligently upon it".[4]

Charles Olson's phrase, "The act of trying to say is always an act of location", is read by the critic Matthew Cooperman as an acknowledgment of the fact that we are always in a place when we create art and our sense of our physical body in the world is the most direct experience of being we have.[5] To me, location of body in place is indeed central and the place I write is almost always outside. Here I am most exposed to all that the outside "location" brings, to what we used to call "nature". My poetry, my "act of trying to say", explores the specificity of the locale and, particularly when I started writing, that was the most important element for me. So my poems were often named after a place – "Brancepeth Beck", "Constantine", "Maine Coast". Often I use local words for natural phenomena, such as the Northern words, "beck" (stream) and "nab" (hill). The "physical body in the world" is also a centre of interest for me. It is in our physical sensations that we may (for a moment) feel ourselves to be just another "curious wandering animal", as Olson puts it in *Human Universe*.[6] It is the closest we come to the non-human world and to wearing away at the deep division between human and non-human that that phrase implies. Like the Platonic division between body and spirit or mind this is just one of a set of powerful dualisms which allow us (dangerously, to my mind) to distinguish ourselves as cultural beings from our own bodies and from nature. The American ecopoet Marcella Durand sums up the great controversy of our status in nature neatly as the "prepositional mystery, whether we are in or of nature".[7]

I am not interested in conducting a cerebral debate about this in my poetry but in embodying the process of engagement and disengagement with the natural world (how it all *feels*) into the writing. For me, Olson's linking of poetic rhythm and form to breath, which I read as literal and associative, is key central both to the writing and the performing of the work. In *"Projective Verse"*, Olson wrote "Verse now, 1950, if it is to be of *essential* use, must, I take it, catch up and put into itself certain laws and possibilities of the breath, of the breathing of the man who writes as well as of his listenings".[8] Apart from the "man who writes" bit, this still speaks to me of the importance of working with human energies and rhythms *as well as* "listening" to those outside ourselves and paying attention to the observed processes of the physical world. These principles were the ones that I brought to my landscape writing of the early '90s and the walking, breathing, moving, writing in the landscape was how I did it. I have never abandoned the site-specific writing that I began at that time, a simple process of visiting, walking and re-visiting, re-walking a place through the seasons. Through this process so much emerges that a drastic editing process is of course crucial.

"Brancepeth Beck", a sequence of fifteen very short poems, was written after walking through a particular valley in Brancepeth, County Durham many times. It is not a coastal poem, but clearly a land and water one, dwelling as it does on the beck which runs through Brancepeth valley.

The emphasis here was very much on sound and energy: rhythm. I am still attached to these poems, but, to me now, they feel a little too "pure", the landscape a little too unmediated.

In this country at least, we have no wilderness left. It's far too late to write romantic pastorals. For better or worse, we (as humanity and as individuals) are implicated in the process by which this has occurred

and, from the mid-nineties onwards, I began to discover and interrogate that implication at the literal level of the land as well as the mental or emotional level of what goes on deep in our unconscious minds. It seemed to me that both the landscape and our own minds were strewn with the relics of our acculturated nature, and many are not so much strewn as buried or unseen, part of the very (polluted) air that circulates around us. I began to explore this in early poems such as *"Constantine"*, a piece which I now feel does not wholly escape sentimentality (one of the difficult legacies of pastoral poetry), but does attempt to reach backwards in time in an act of historical imagination.[9] I set out to find the ancient church and well at Constantine Bay in North Cornwall with an Ordinance Survey map only to find it was actually on the golf course, the very one that Mrs Thatcher and Denis used to helicopter on to from London. I evoked the archeological layers, the ruins and features, of a site once cultural, now naturalised, but also included data from other "found" sources, people's speech, signposts, and reference to other evidence of human intervention. This is a practise I have continued, attempting to move the poetry beyond the restricted poet/landscape context, for instance later hill and moor poems make reference to farming, building work, bowls players, the school run and other rural or semi-rural social activity in landscape.

This is part of my resistance to the romantic role of the traditional pastoral poet, of attempting to minimise what Olson, taking his cue from the Objectivists, described as the "lyrical interference of the individual as ego".[10] In using the word "lyrical" Olson conjures up the "I" upon "I" upon "I" of lyric poetry's past. I have not banned the lyric "I", the voice of the poet, from my work; to make it entirely invisible feels fraudulent to me. Rather, I explore it and undermine it, holding it back from egotistical domination or ownership of landscape, exploring its collusion with cultural, social and environmental constructs and practises. Presence and influence cuts both ways. Over ten years ago now, in *"Writing Outside"*, I wrote that, "to take on the pastoral tradition is to face immediately a homocentric and egocentric centre to the poet's role and to displace that is a matter of walking out of the impossible".[11] I still feel that but, these days, the pastoral battle does not matter quite so much to me. I am not so distressed when my own critical formulation "radical landscape poetry" is misquoted "radical pastoral poetry", and I am described as writing it! This seems to me now to imply a playful, deconstructive attitude to pastoral, but, crucially, not to deny the pastoral's significance, both in terms of our cultural attitudes and our poetic history.

As my references to relics being both literal and cultural imply, I am interested in the desires we all locate in nature, desires I attempted to embody and explore in my work, be they about wanting locality as a rooting in a tamed, contained earth or the desire for an encounter with wilderness or the need to own through knowledge and classification or the romantic desire to be overwhelmed, for epiphany or merging with nature. All of these are frames which restrict and sometimes exploit, as well as powerful forces which we can use. Like all mythologies, we need to understand them.

The poem in which I first explored this was called "Love/Land" but it emerges through all my recent sequence work in particular "Coast" (written on the North Cornish coast through the process of walking between Trevone and Padstow at various times of year) and "Nab" which is based on a similar walking and re-walking of Cheesegate Nab in the Holme Valley. I tried to write the rhythms of desire and the rhythms of the season and the body into this work.

I've been using phrases like "outside" and "landscape" in this essay, but only one word has to be changed for my whole piece to shift a gear. If I were to talk about the human relationship to the "environment", a whole new set of associations emerges. We no longer feel that the environment is our playground in which to experience a series of romantic and/or erotic associations and feelings such as the Romantic poets might have felt comfortable with. We no longer feel that natural phenomena from the English summer rain shower to the Asian tsunami, the unexpected hot spell in April to the drought in Southern Africa, are in fact natural, the visitations of nature, nor even of fate or the gods. Suddenly what was powerful becomes fragile and our sense of guilty responsibility becomes harder and harder to evade. I've been trying to write that in to my more recent poems, to register the significance of the environmental crisis and, perhaps more significantly given the place of the poet, to explore how this changes our relationship to landscape. This enters all manner of my poems these days. I recently accepted a commission to write a poem about climate change, the first time in my writing life I have ever agreed to write "about" anything. Why, as a poet who is more concerned with form than content, with language more than themes, did I agree? It was precisely because I feel the need now to explore how our language of environment, of nature, of landscape and locale, is changing and with it our whole relationship to the world outside ourselves, the world that is perhaps no longer outside ourselves at all. Eco-critics such as Jhan Hochman have questioned the word "environment". Hochman has noted that "environment" has come to mean "nature only tangibly important to human health or livelihood", the world as it serves us, a part of the dominant "chronic, excessive anthropocentrism".[12] I envisage this as the earth wrapped around us, a comfort blanket of resources, electricity, coal, power, fuel, water, light. In all the talk about the eco-system, the complex inter-related network of natural resources that environmentalists and ecologists have explored, perhaps it is not too late to realise that this system actually includes us, rather than simply serving us, as the Judaeo-Christian tradition would once have had us believe. So, in writing poetry, I long ago went beyond the idea that a poem, like a traditional story, might simply be set in a recognisable place where that place functions merely as background. I have been more interested in reaching a form of writing in which we say more about our relationship to our environment as an individual but also as a society. Even, at the far reaches of imagination, might the place, the environment, the non-human inhabitants become more of an active protagonist in the work? This is my new direction, old and new. It has always been there, but today it has a very different significance and stress. "Land and relic" has a rather romantic, appealing ring to it. "Land *as* relic", perhaps not so much, yet, already, in the Southern African drought-ridden countries, ecologists talk of desertification; where rain forests were, they speak of deforestation; where coral reef eco-systems flourished, they talk of "coral mortality" and "mass bleaching". These are ugly words for a poet to have to encounter, and the response to them is not so easy to find…

catching against
breaking
branch
thick pulling
bramble
steady hand
stinging sharp
leaves
down slip mud
through cold
swaying
flowers deep
moon trees squared
lightwindows

thrilling dove takes
airsound   thrilling
dove takes air
sound   sheep
and below sheep
aircry under
i breathing blue
below branches
new night rain
colour

hiding dig
low hish under
river bed beck
damming up
di ver ting
day/may time
high rises
overbanks

headland, island, rock,
                        carn on land, carn on island
sequences of rock

small standing
                never to see it all
just light and dark, tide up or down,

it's not quite   not there
        a level change, a cave
                    overlapping head
                    a halftide rock didn't know
when we didn't see it   a cormorant
                                a fracture, join and shift

take the map away,
you might believe your eyes

you'd never know, my love
where   you are

and if
that silver line
is the horizon lift

white catching-light, stonechats blurring call

and lift

before life

crying
up a high strand

cave   womb in womb   cliff

                                    white-gold pup
wet under   shadows
                 under steep
lichens
old gold and green
       under all that island
                                        crying
                                        up a high strand

mother dark silver
leaf-thick
current

pulls   above cave drips
sun   down
                                          to

       rock, purple

Pappus

banks of purple thistle ragwort rosebay
                                        all spread white
purple pink yellow
sowthistle
all but gone

                                up a high horizon
mist shift perspective
                                        can't see
anyone but you

                                        watching
feathering fruit

                                        very changeable
white of

                                        a turning tide
letting fly

we feel
sea drags us
under   mist
                                moves   white seed
                                                        on white
                                                        takes air

        and it's wind moon time

a caught force
in white haze

are we

rosebay, thistle, ragwort
know to

disperse

From "throwing it all away" [15]

throwing
away   easy

into the street
pint after pint after pint

                                or oranges
                                    turning
impeding infirmities

until there's enough room
for us all

                        fresh to squeeze and cut

tape measure falling from her skirt

catching the quick way out

                        certain areas on the east coast
                        are not worth saving
                        let the sea come in

sweeping earth up
feeding it back
to the next one
shaking dead roots
free never throwing
away when the sack
breeds old hair and
blood back any
way

NOTES

[1] Harriet Tarlo, 'Writing Outside', *Foil: defining poetry 1985-2000*, ed. Nicholas Johnson, etruscan books, 2000.

[2] Jack Foley, 'Projective Verse at 50', *Flashpoint* (Winter 2001): Web Issue 4, http://www.flashpointmag.com/projvers.htm; Kathleen Fraser, *translating the unspeakable: poetry and the innovative necessity*, Tuscaloosa and London: The University of Alabama Press, 2000, 175.

[3] Duncan referred to open form writing as 'the opening of the field' and this was the title of his 1960 volume of poetry (Robert Duncan, *The Opening of the Field*, New York: Grove Press, 1960)..

[4] Harriet Tarlo, 'Radical Landscapes: experiment and environment in contemporary poetry' *Jacket* 32 (April 2007), http://jacketmagazine.com/32/index.shtml. For more detailed discussion of individual poets see Harriet Tarlo, 'Radical British Landscape Poetry in the Bunting Tradition', *The Star You Steer By: Basil Bunting and British Modernism*, ed. R. Price and J. McGonigal, Editions Rodopi, 2000.

[5] Matthew Cooperman, 'Charles Olson: Archaeologist of Morning, Ecologist of Evening' in Tallmadge, John and Harrington, Henry, *Reading Under the Sign of Nature: New Essays in Ecocriticism*, Salt Lake City: The University of Utah Press, 2000.

[6] Charles Olson, 'Human Universe', *The New Writing in the USA*, eds. Donald Allen and Robert Creeley, Middlesex: Penguin, 1967, p188.

[7] Marcella Durand, 'Spatial Interpretations: Ways of Reading Ecological Poetry' in Reilly, Evelyn, and Ijima, Brenda. *((eco(lang) (uage (reader))*. Portable Press at Yo Yo Labs (www.yoyolabs.com), forthcoming 2008 Fall 2007.

[8] Charles Olson, 'Projective Verse', *The Poetics of the New American Poetry*, ed. Donald M. Allen and Warren Tallman, New York, Grove Press, 1973.

[9] Harriet Tarlo, *Poems 1990-2003*, Shearsman Press, 2004, p93-8.

[10] Charles Olson, 'Projective Verse', *The Poetics of the New American Poetry*, ed. Donald M. Allen and Warren Tallman, New York, Grove Press, 1973, 156.

[11] Harriet Tarlo, 'Writing Outside', *Foil: defining poetry 1985-2000*, ed. Nicholas Johnson, etruscan books, 2000.

[12] Jhan Hochman, 'Green Cultural Studies: An Introductory Critique of an Emerging Discipline', *Mosaic* 30:1 (1997), extracted in Laurence Coupe, *The Green Studies Reader from Romanticism to Ecocriticism*, London and New York: Routledge, 2000, p 188.

[13] Harriet Tarlo, 'Brancepeth Beck', The Other Press, 1997, reprinted in Nab *(Brancepeth Beck, Coast and Nab)*, etruscan books, 2005.

[14] Harriet Tarlo, *Love/Land*, Cambridge: REM Press, 2003.

[15] *Poems 1990-2003*, Shearsman Press, 2004, p23.

Guy Moreton

Landscape as mindscape:
searching for a place to think

This paper will discuss two recent and interrelated projects. W.G Sebald's fictive wanderings through the East Anglian landscape in The Rings of Saturn are the starting point for photographs made by Guy Moreton and presented in the exhibition Waterlog with artists Tacita Dean, Marcus Coates, Alec Finlay, Simon Pope and Alexander and Susan Maris. Wanderings and sojourns were also central in Ludwig Wittgenstein's search for a place to write. For many years he travelled to Skjolden on the west coast of Norway where he lived in a remote house overlooking Lake Eidsvatnet at the inner end of the Sognefjord. The motif of the architectural ruin and the suggestion of melancholy in these landscapes of quiet seriousness are explored throughout Moreton's practice.

This paper considers two recent and interrelated projects: *Waterlog* and *Ludwig Wittgenstein – There Where You Are Not.*

Dunwich, with its towers and many thousand souls, has dissolved into water, sand and thin air. If you look out from the cliff-top across the sea towards where the town must once have been, you can sense the immense power of emptiness.
W. G. Sebald, The Rings of Saturn 1998

W.G Sebald's melancholic wanderings through the East Anglian landscape in his novel/memoir/travelogue *The Rings of Saturn* are the starting point for a series of photographs made for the exhibition *Waterlog*. These photographs, however, stem from my own distant, fragmented memories and almost parallel journeys. As a postgraduate student in Norwich in 1997, I often used to walk along Dunwich Beach with a German artist friend who lived in Suffolk. I remember vividly the walk along the shingle beach, before we climbed up onto the heath and walked back through the woods, past the ruins of the Grey Friars monastery and the last surviving gravestone from All Saints' churchyard. We lost touch towards the end of 2001. In 1999 I lived in Rotterdam, as an artist in residence, and travelled through the landscape of South Holland: in particular the low-lying waterlogged marshes called *Het Verdronken Landschap*, or *The Drowned Landscape*. Like the narrator of *The Rings of Saturn*, I visited the Mauritshuis to see the paintings of Rembrandt, Breughel, Van Ruisdael and Vermeer; walked the marshes of Haddiscoe and Reedham and visited Somerleyton.[1]

My return to Dunwich for *Waterlog* was in collaboration with the artist and poet Alec Finlay. I had recounted my stories of Dunwich walks to Alec including the myth of church bells chiming from under the sea at low tide – myths that are not uncommon in other parts of the east coast of England that have succumbed to the overwhelming

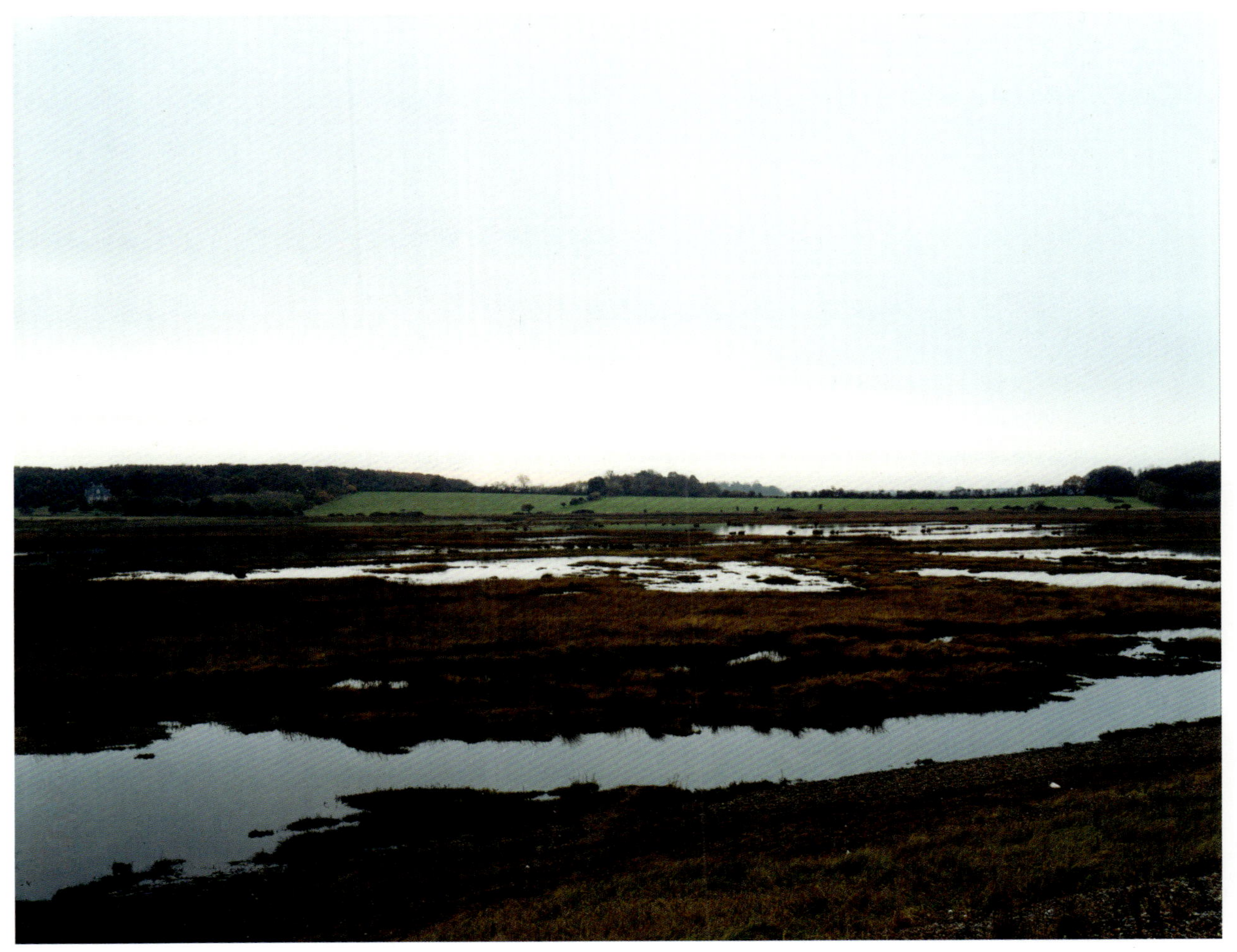

Dingle Marsh
Dunwich 2007
c-print 105x132cm

force of the sea. The town was one of the most important ports in medieval England, and may have possessed as many as eighteen churches, chapels and religious buildings. The last church to fall over the cliffs was *All Saints* on 12th November 1919, as the narrator in *The Rings of Saturn* notes, 'together with the bones of those buried in the graveyard'. We knew that All Saints had a small peal of bells, inherited from the church of *Saint Peter* before it fell to the sea in 1688. This then became the basis for the exhibition: Alec made a poem-card and a series of thirteen watercolour spot paintings called *The Sunken Bell* transcribing the bell method *Plain Bob Minor* representing what was possibly the last rung peal in Dunwich from the seventeenth century. My colour photographs of the ruined chancel of the parish church of Walberswick sat alongside the paintings. Walberswick grew as Dunwich declined in the fourteenth and fifteenth centuries, and much of the wealth of the new town was most obviously reflected in the building of this church. It was common practice in some medieval churches for the Sanctus bell to be located in the Chancel, and was rung at the consecration during Mass. Arvo Pärt's Cantus in *Memorium Benjamin Britten*[2] written in response to the death of Benjamin Britten in 1976 uses the bell as a musical trace, as *tintinnabulation*. The artists Alexander and Susan Maris made the beautifully elegaic film *Silentium*[3] that takes the viewer on a journey upriver towards Snape and to Chapel House – Benjamin Britten's home on the Suffolk coast, south of Walberswick and Dunwich where one might imagine he too was surrounded by a tintinnabular sea.

Had Sebald continued his *English Pilgrimage*[4] further north around the east coast, he might have reached the ruin of Dunston Pillar, Britain's only land lighthouse, built in 1751 to guide travellers through the then treacherous heathlands and marshes of south Lincolnshire. It is situated close to the city of Lincoln, where I was born and lived until the age of six. I made three photographs of the pillar: two that circled a distant view of the ruined tower on the horizon from the East and from the West, and one detail of the entrance to the lighthouse – perhaps the final destination for the eighteenth century traveller.

Wanderings and sojourns were also central in Ludwig Wittgenstein's search for a place to write. For many years he travelled to Skjolden on the west coast of Norway where he lived in a remote house overlooking Lake Eidsvatnet at the inner end of the Sognefjord at different periods in his life, from 1913 until his death in 1951. I started working on this project initially with the idea of making a bookwork, as a collaboration with the artist and poet Alec Finlay in 2001. We travelled to Skjolden in Norway together in 2001 and 2002 and originally envisaged a purely visual study of the surrounding landscape, made as an artist book. The photographs that I made, however, were exhibited in the John Hansard Gallery Southampton in 2005 in the exhibition *There Where You Are Not*. The book evolved into an album of photographic sketches and a poem-collage and was published by Black Dog Publishing in late 2005 as *Ludwig Wittgenstein – There Where You Are Not*.

Our intention was artistic rather than biographical. Together we attempted to uncover something of the extraordinary character of the landscape of Skjolden and, in doing so, to reveal the contemplative side of Wittgenstein. The landscapes of 'quiet seriousness' Wittgenstein

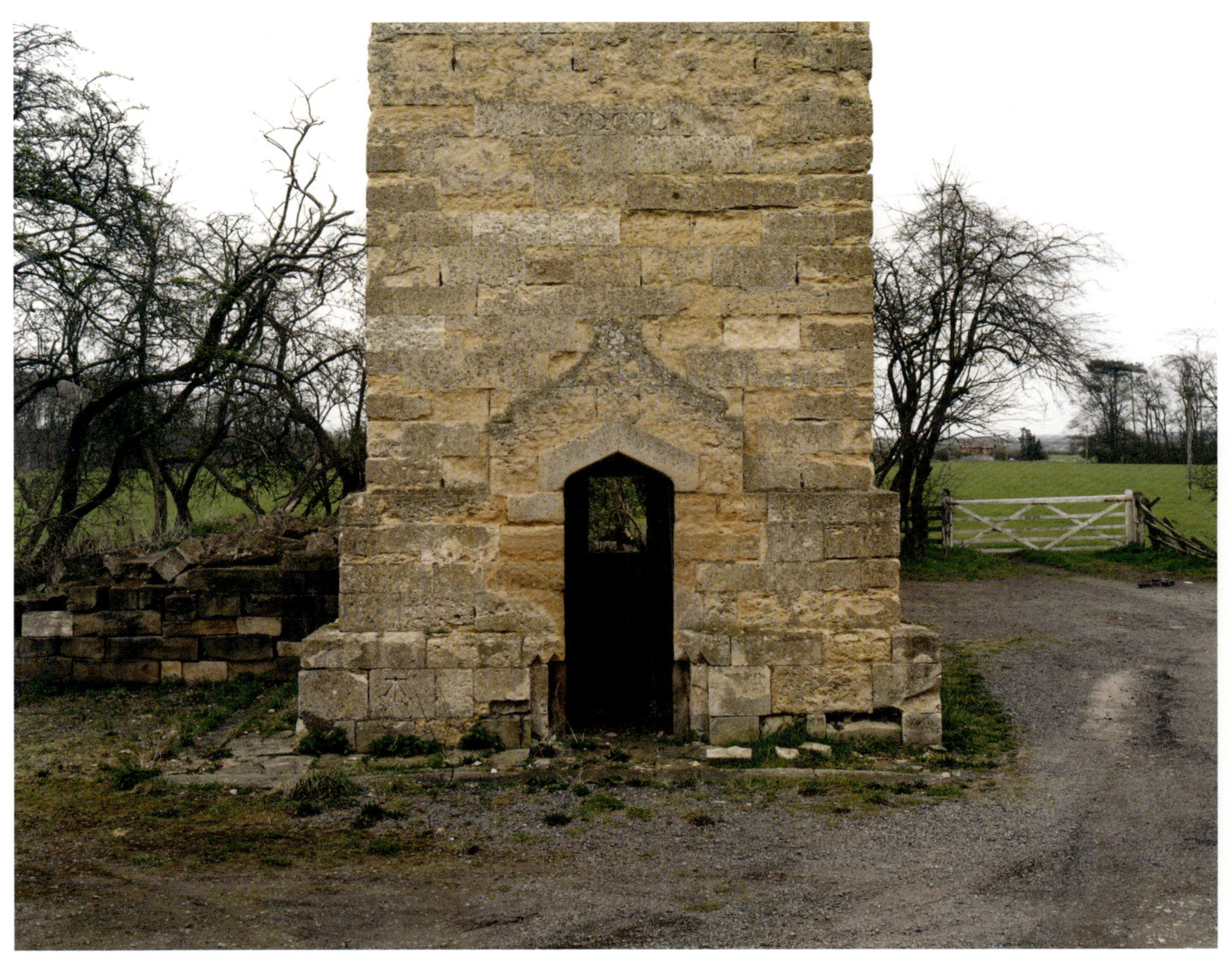

Dunston Pillar
(detail) 2007,
c-print 105x132cm

found in Norway and Ireland represent his lifelong search for a place where he could work. Importantly, they also reflect the character of his thought.

> In Skjolden he could be free from such conflicts; he could be himself without the strain of upsetting or offending people. It was a tremendous liberation. He could devote himself entirely to himself – or, rather, to what he felt to be practically the same thing, to his logic. That and the beauty of the countryside – ideal for the long , solitary walks he needed as both relaxation and a meditation – produced in him a kind of euphoria. Together they created the perfect conditions in which to think.
> Ray Monk, Ludwig Wittgenstein – The Duty of Genius 1990

The book was much extended as a result of meeting Michael Nedo, the editor of the 'Vienna Edition' of Wittgenstein's writings and director of The Wittgenstein Archive, Cambridge. Michael suggested the importance of elevated outlooks that have lent a distinctive topography to Wittgenstein's thinking, from the family home in Vienna, the country estate, the Hochreit, to K10 Wittgenstein's room with a view over the rooftops in Whewell's Court, Trinity College Cambridge. The importance of an elevated outlook was made physically manifest in the particular situation and positioning of the small house in Skjolden, built on stone foundations and on its own above the lake some way up a mountainside looking west towards the village and Lustrafjord in the distance. Unusual for a Norwegian house of this kind, the gable and veranda faced the lake, much like a Swiss or Austrian Alpine chalet. The house was dismantled in the 1960s, and rebuilt in the village and is now privately owned. The rock foundations are what is left – a small plateau on the west coast of Norway that stands for the possibility of creative thought.

> A picture held us captive and we could not get outside it.
> Ludwig Wittgenstein, Philosophical Investigations 1953

My photographs were made in a process that I consider akin to the methodology of drawing and the idea of a picture-construct that not only describes but also, and perhaps paradoxically, uncovers something of the complexity of ordinary thought. Inherent in this process is a particular attention to seeing – to view-finding – followed by a slow process of clarification of the inverted picture within its rectangular frame. Walking was intrinsic to the work, allowing a physical context and rhythm to the project that also enabled a thought-process; a layering of time and of context. The lush green pastoral landscape and forest was also the stage and backdrop in Knut Hamsun's novel *Pan* – where the lead protagonist Thomas Glahn yearns for, amongst other things, a simple life. This recurring motif of the retreat or repose, particularly in the west coast of Norway where the 'simple' or philosophical life was chosen not just by Wittgenstein, but also by Kurt Schwitters who spent much of his time in the 1930s living in a primitive woodshed on the island of Hjertøya near Molde. Per Kirkeby's essay *Schwitters in Norway* and reproductions of Schwitters' somewhat nostalgic paintings

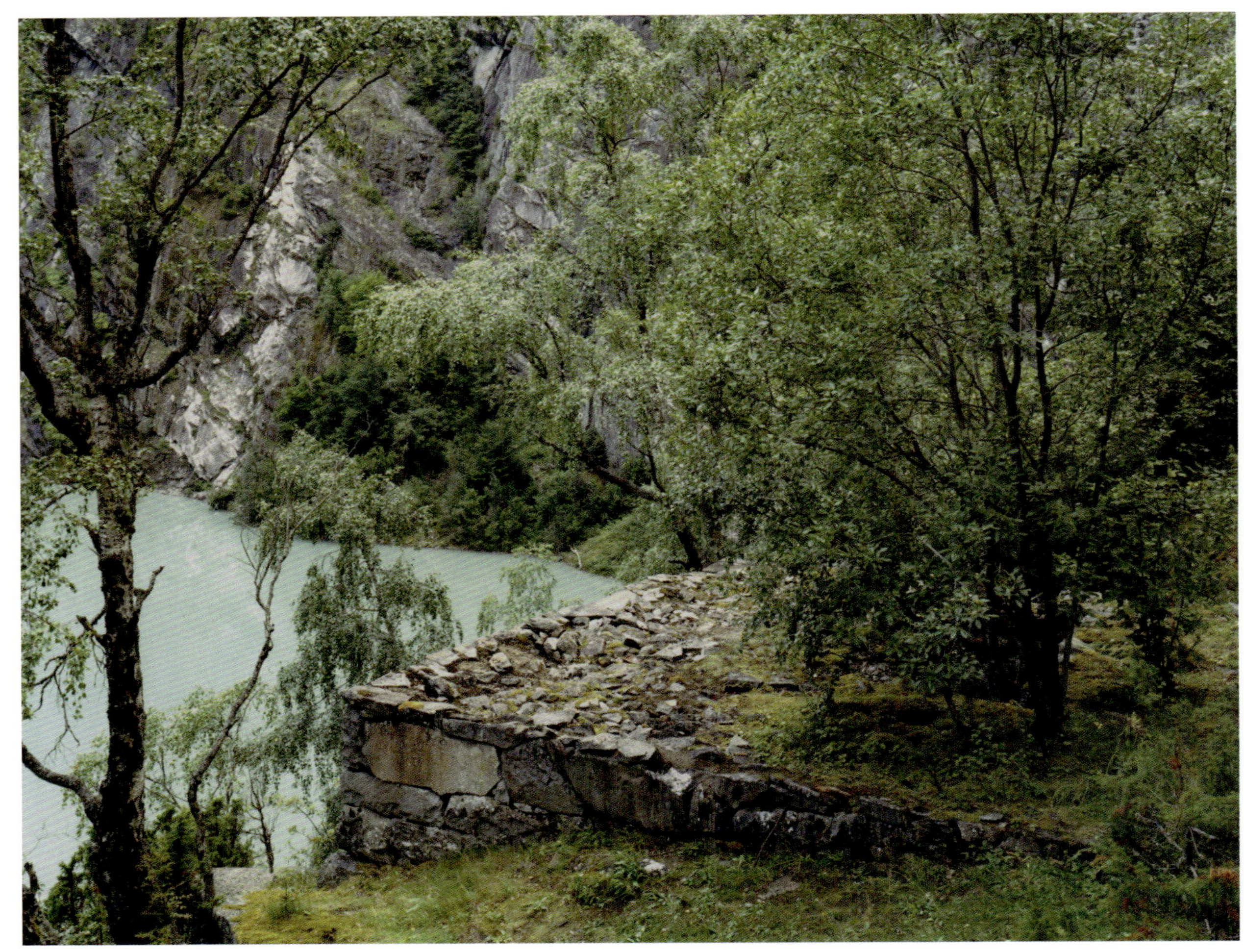

LW 118 Skjolden *2001*
c-print 105x132cm

of the landscape around the island and particularly his depictions of the vernacular architecture within the landscape acted as a prelude and parallel literary journey to my photographs in *There Where You Are Not*, and as such felt an important counter.

The idea of the relic is important here too – the photograph of the rock foundations where Ludwig Wittgenstein's house once overlooked the fjord, also stands as a cultural relic that somehow enables us to step outside of ourselves and return the canonical modernist gaze of melancholy over and above the brooding circle of mountains that surrounds us. Schwitters' constant journeying between Hanover and Molde, between the Avant-Garde milieu in 1930s Germany and sojourns at his island paradise in Hjertøya were interspersed with work on a new *Merzbau* at Lysaker near Oslo, before the situation in Germany and then Norway became too dangerous eventually forcing Schwitters to flee Norway for England. Sebald's place as a writer is now firmly embedded somewhere in this journey too. To go full circle back to my photograph of the ruin of Dunston Pillar in the flat Lincolnshire landscape, one is confronted with an ornate entrance that frames a small square window. This in turn frames not only the physical wilderness of dense tree branches and fields in the distance, but also perhaps frames the idea of *Land and Relic* – that as readers we collectively inhabit the character of the traveller mapping a place somewhere between the wandering unconscious mind and the architectural relic, or between wilderness and culture. In this case the relic might stand for the nature of time itself, about 'our capacity to drift from one place, one history or one subject to another and still have no notion how we navigated the darkness in between.'[5]

BIBLIOGRAPHY

Steven Bode and Nina Ernst, *Waterlog: Journeys Around An Exhibition*, Film and Video Umbrella London 2007

Knut Hamsun, *Pan*, Penguin Books 1998 (translated into English by Sverre Lyngstad)

Per Kirkeby, *Schwitters*, Edition Bløndal 1995

Ray Monk, *Ludwig Wittgenstein: The Duty of Genius,* Jonathan Cape 1990

Michael Nedo, *Ludwig Wittgenstein: Wiener Ausgabe* Introduction Springer-Verlag Vienna and New York 1993

Michael Nedo, Guy Moreton, Alec Finlay: *Ludwig Wittgenstein – There Where You Are Not,* London: Black Dog Publishing 2005

W.G Sebald, *The Rings of Saturn* London: The Harvill Press 1998 (translated from German by Michael Hulse)

W.G Sebald and Jan Peter Tripp, *Unrecounted* London: Hamish Hamilton 2004 (translated by Michael Hamburger)

Ludwig Wittgenstein, *Philosophical Investigations* Oxford: Blackwell 1976

Ludwig Wittgenstein, *Tractatus Logico-Philosophicus* Routledge Classics 2001

NOTES

[1] Haddiscoe and Reedham are villages in Norfolk, situated on the edge of the Norfolk Broads between Norwich and Great Yarmouth. Somerleyton is a village in north-east Suffolk that also overlooks the tributaries of rivers and lakes that form the Norfolk Broads. See Sebald's The Rings of Saturn p.30/31

[2] Arvo Pärt: *Tabula Rasa*, ECM Records New Series 1988

[3] See *Waterlog: Journeys Around an Exhibition* Ed. Steven Bode, Nina Ernst and Jeremy Millar. Film and Video Umbrella London 2007.

[4] The original German title for W. G Sebald's *The Rings of Saturn* was 'Die Ringe des Saturn: Eine Englische Wallfahrt' (1995).

[5] See Brian Dillon's essay 'Airlocked' in *Waterlog: Journeys Around an Exhibition*, Film and Video Umbrella London 2007

ZINEB SEDIRA

Saphir

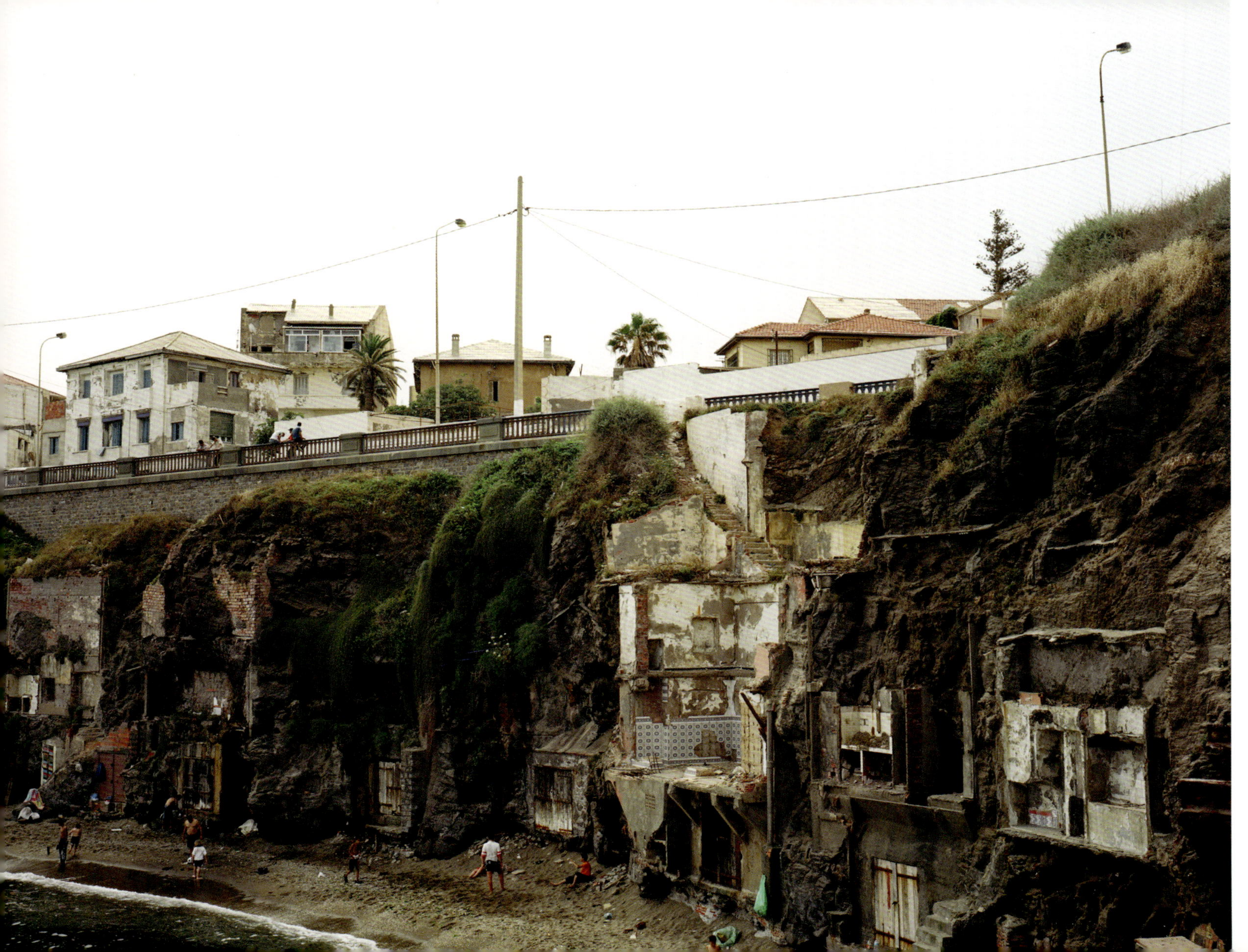

This latest project from Zineb Sedira entitled Saphir is a series of photographs and a two-screen video projection, shot in and around the port of Algiers. Concentrating on the landscape and architecture which gives Algiers its particular Western allure, Saphir directs the gaze and the mind toward the Mediterranean that separates Algeria from France. Confronting the contemporary life of the city with an older and more ambivalent legacy, the project Saphir presents a portrait of Algiers in a transitional moment, the local character gradually becoming absorbed into the current of increasing globalization.

Previously, my work was concerned with issues of language and storytelling using photography and video. The work was about my family experience of immigrating to France from Algeria, my growing up in Paris and my move to England in 1986. I was interested in how my parents talked about their Algerian culture and its history. This led me to creat a body of work exploring oral history. The style of filming was documentary and experimental using an interview format. They were interior shots and languages spoken by my family (English, French and Arabic) were explored in the works.

In 2003, my art practice took a new direction due to my return to Algeria after 15 years of absence because of the civil war. This influenced my work deeply, provoking a new body of work about the landscape of Algeria.

As I was now able to film and photograph locally I developed worked around the landscape of Algiers and its architecture.

The works - as previously - deals with mobility and colonial legacies. However, it is shot in external spaces as opposed to a photographic studio or my parent's house thus allowing me to create new imagery and use film.

Also, as an artist, I travel frequently so I began to explore places of departure and arrival such as airports, seaports and train stations. This, of course, ties in with the issues previously explored: my parent's migration and their subsequent return to Algeria as well as my own 'immigration' to London.

The Mediterranean Sea became the centre of recent pieces of work. It lies between France and Algeria and is a site of historical, cultural and contemporary 'movement' but also a connection and separation between South and North.

"And the road goes on…" is a video created in 2005 and was commissioned by Beaconsfield Gallery.

Algeria is rarely portrayed in the UK and on the occasions that it is the reference is negatively centred upon tales of civil unrest, terrorism and massacre. It is located between the tourist destinations of Morocco and Tunisia, and larger than both, yet, the culture and landscape of Algeria remains an unknown country, especially for England.

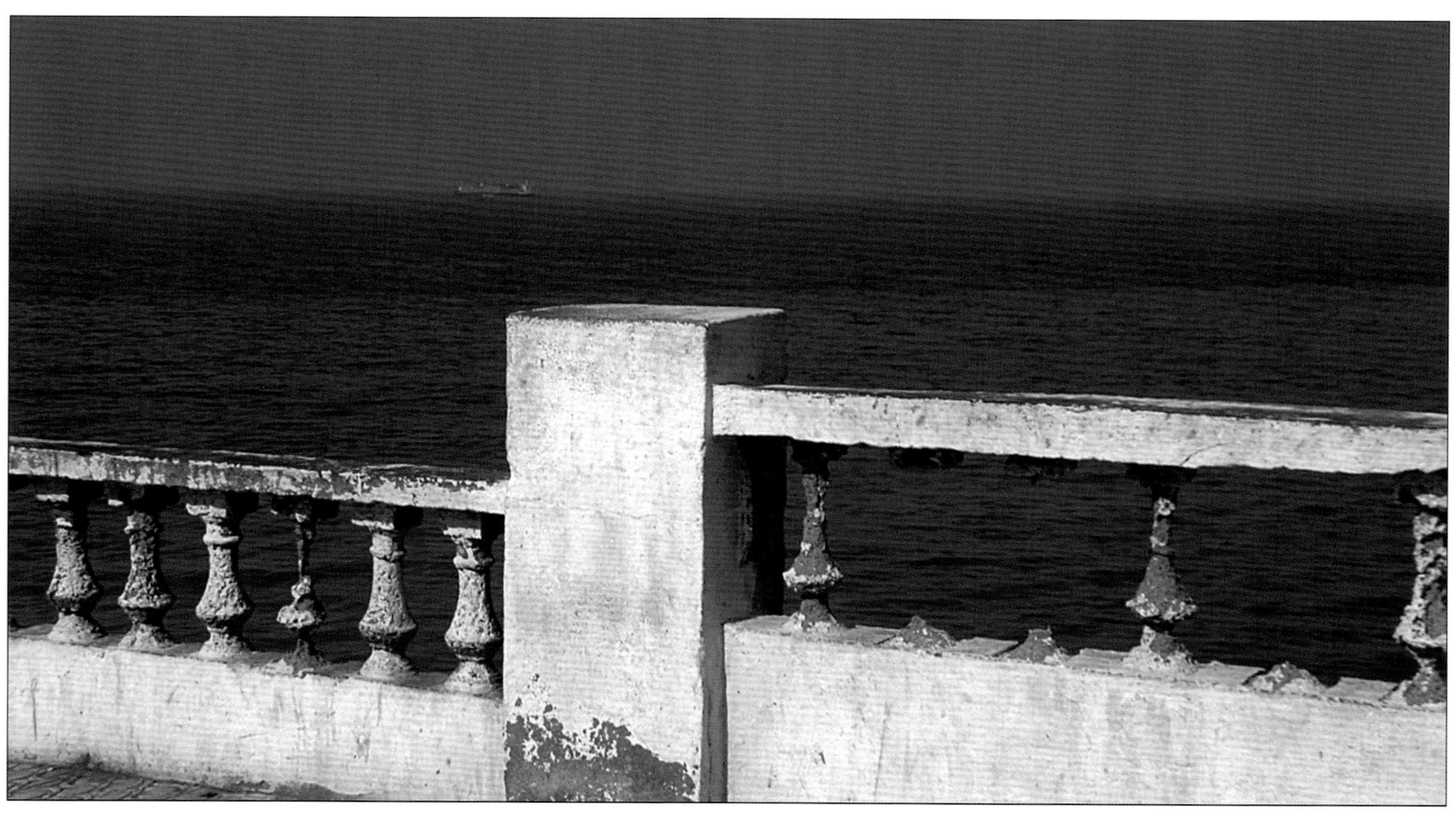

Framing the view, *2006 (previous left hand page)*
c-print
76 x 50 cm

Saphir, *2006 (this page and right)*
Video installation with two projections in 16:9,
18 minutes

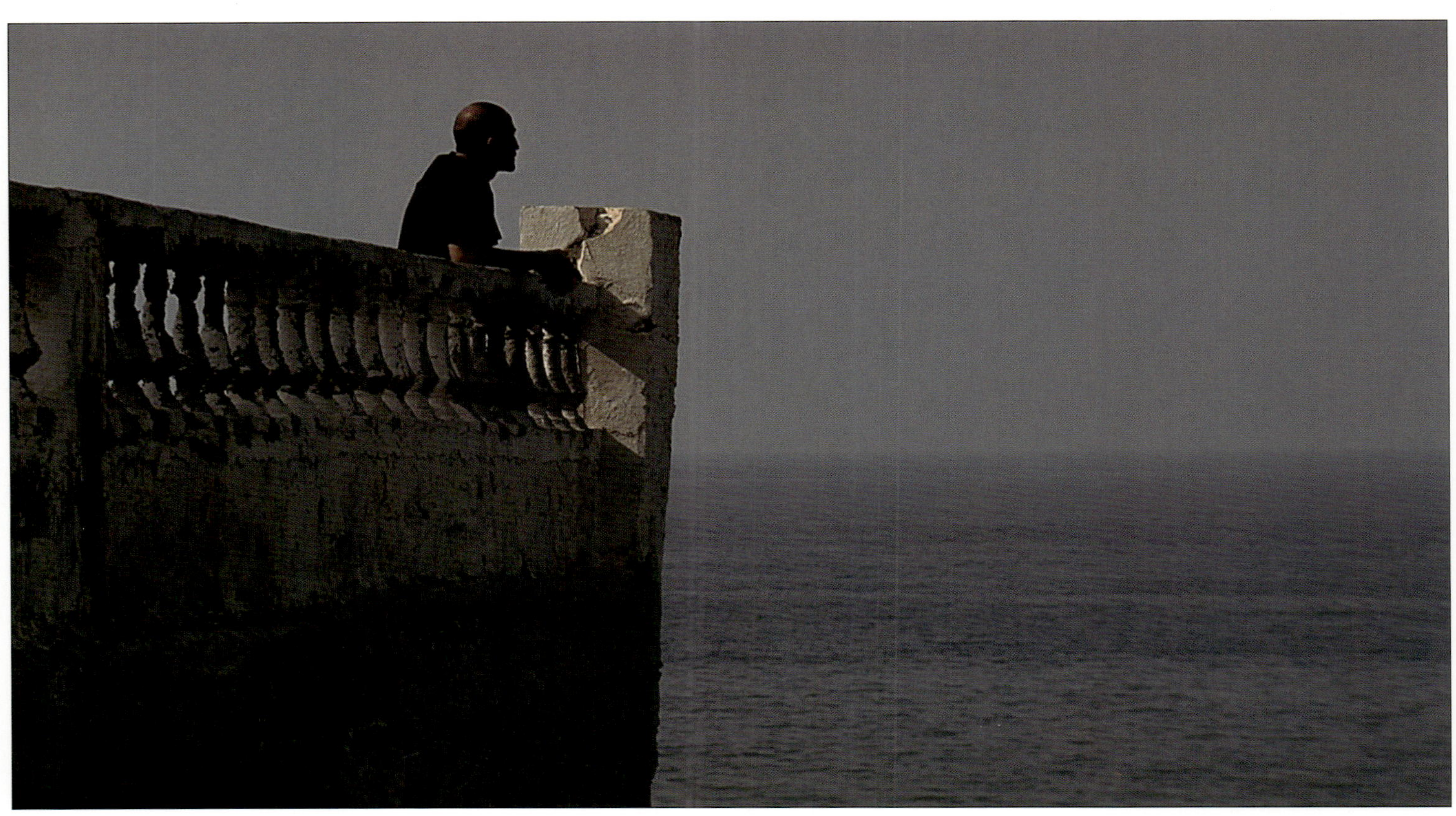

In France, it is a very different situation because of the colonial history of the two countries.

'*And the road goes on…*' is a re-discovery of Algeria. The travelogue focuses upon the incidence of human presence in a stunning natural setting, drawing the spectator into an inviting space. Yet, the work presents an aspect of the country in its day to day normality.

The film is slowed down at certain moments - focussing on a passer-by or man on a bicycle - and the gaze of the viewer is heightened as people and moments, which ordinarily would not be noticed when in a moving car, become still and woven into the landscape.

The video offers a curious inversion questioning time, space and movement. The landscape, usually immobile, flies by at an absurd speed, while humans, who are usually moving, remain static.

In September 2006, the French curator Christine Van Assche (chief curator of new media at the Pompidou Centre) was invited to curate an exhibition at the Photographers Gallery as part of the Paris Calling festival. The aim of the festival was to give exposure to French artists. She invited me to exhibit there. The curator was interested in inviting a French artist of Algerian origins living in London in order to question what it means to be a French artist.

Concurrently, Film and Video Umbrella offered to commission a new film, which we agreed to exhibit at the Photographer's Gallery for Paris Calling. This opportunity to create new work led me to think about what it means to be French, Algerian and based in London. As a product of that legacy I decided to revisit the French-Algerian relationship, looking at movement between places.

I created *Saphir* during summer 2006. The video develops a dialogue between the sea, two protagonists and a colonial hotel situated in the port of Algiers. A dynamic is set up between the two protagonists and the sea as the site of both connection and separation. These binaries are explored throughout the film using a combination of framing and precisely timed fade-ins and fade-outs, along with the exploitation of the dual screen presentation.

The port of Algiers became the stage where notions of arrival and departure, stasis and transition, belonging and not belonging were played out.

Accompanying *Saphir* at the Photographer's Gallery, I produced a series of photographs about the impact of French colonialism on the Algerian landscape and architecture. Some of these colonial buildings became a strong theme in *Framing the View and Haunted House*. One can see dilapidated houses emerging out of cliffs where they once stood overlooking the sea. With this in mind, Algiers's coastline appears as a point of transition between east and west, memory and oblivion, the past and the present.

Although ravaged by time and the sea, the constructions are neither cared for nor demolished.

Today its facade seems to ask the question: "What will become of these French colonial ruins? Will they eventually turn to dust amid widespread indifference? Or, in a few centuries will they become a symbol of national pride like the sites that bear witness to the hegemony of Rome during Antiquity?

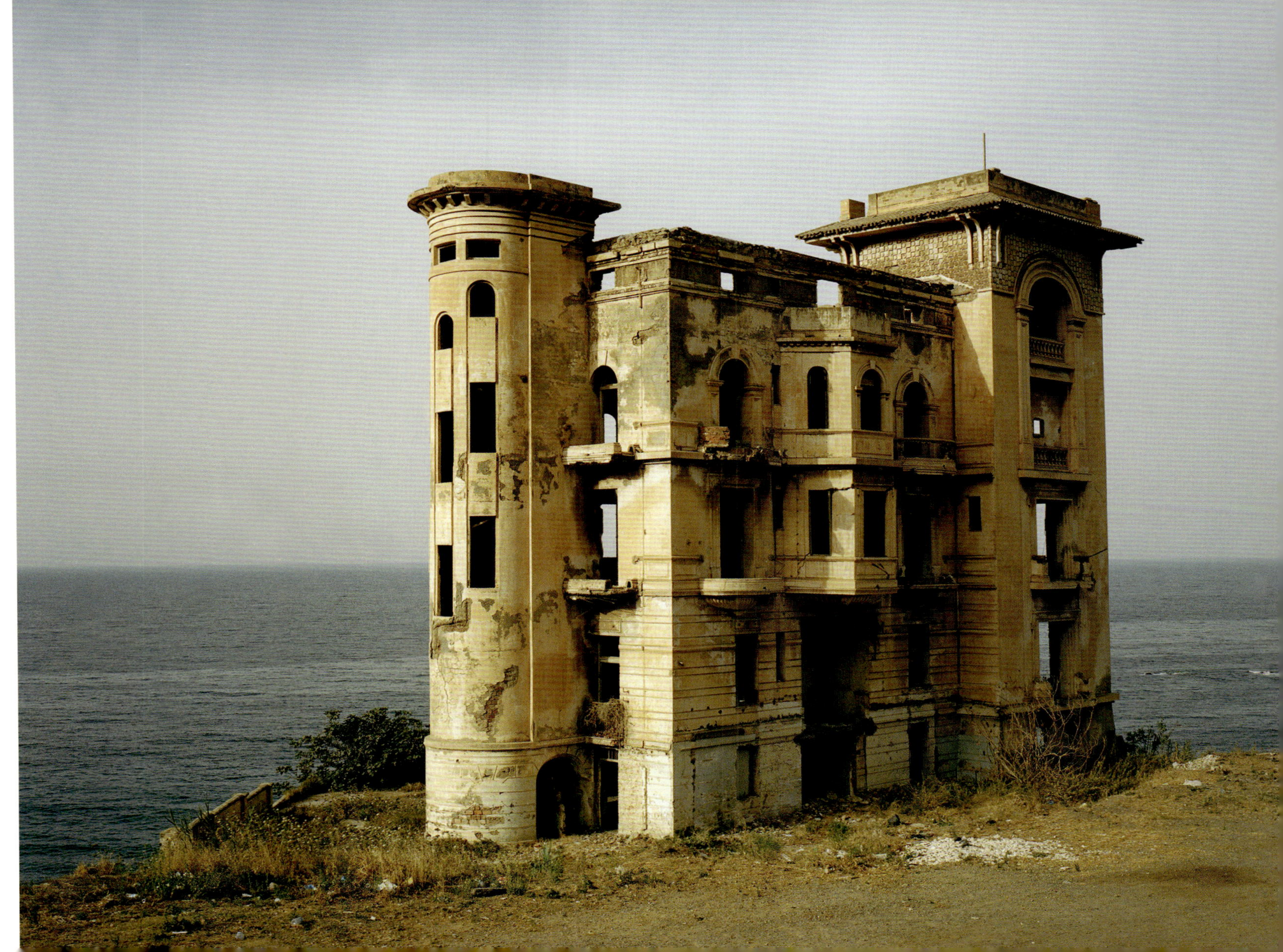

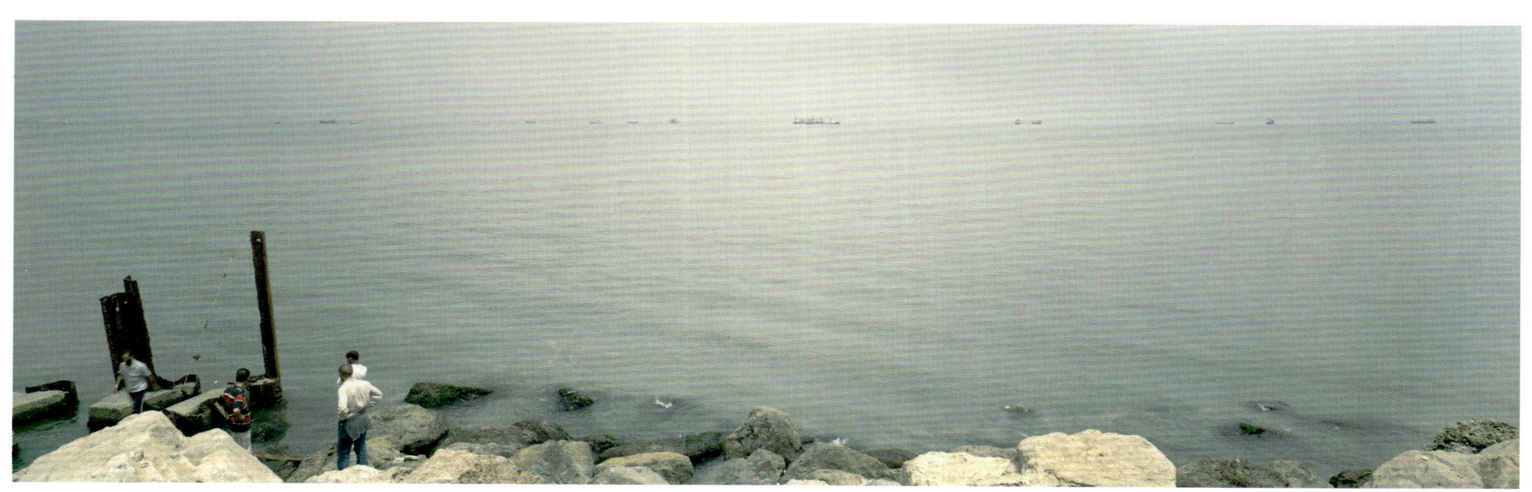

Transitional landscape, *2006*
Panoramic c-prints
150 x 75 cm

Haunted House, *2006 (previous right hand page)*
c-print
100 x 80 cm

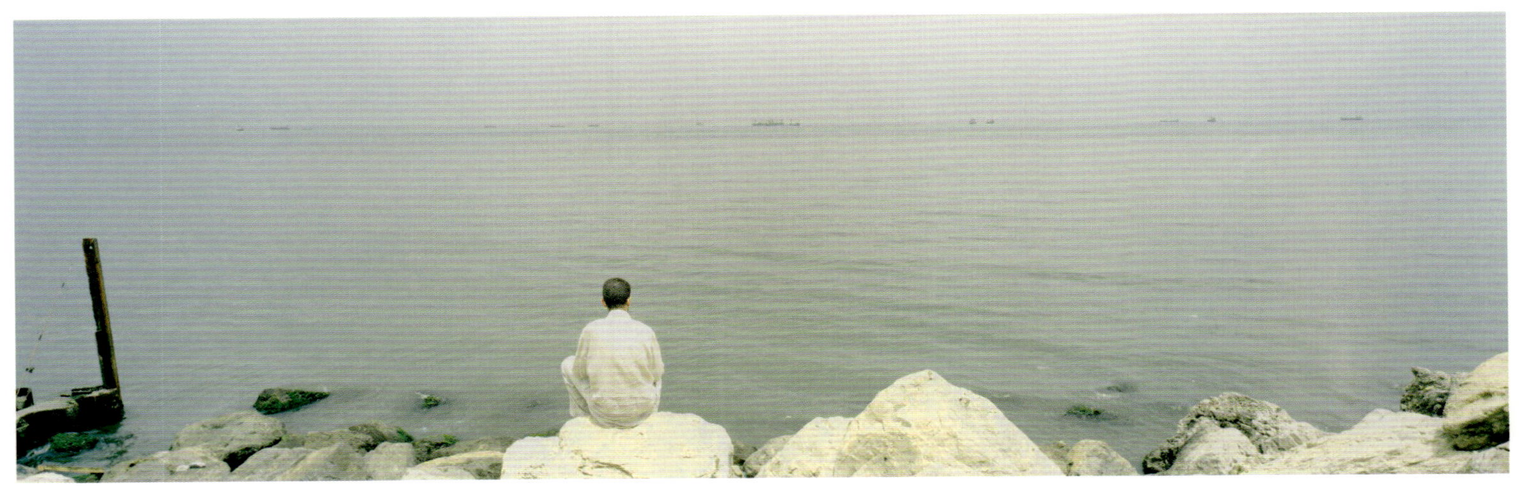

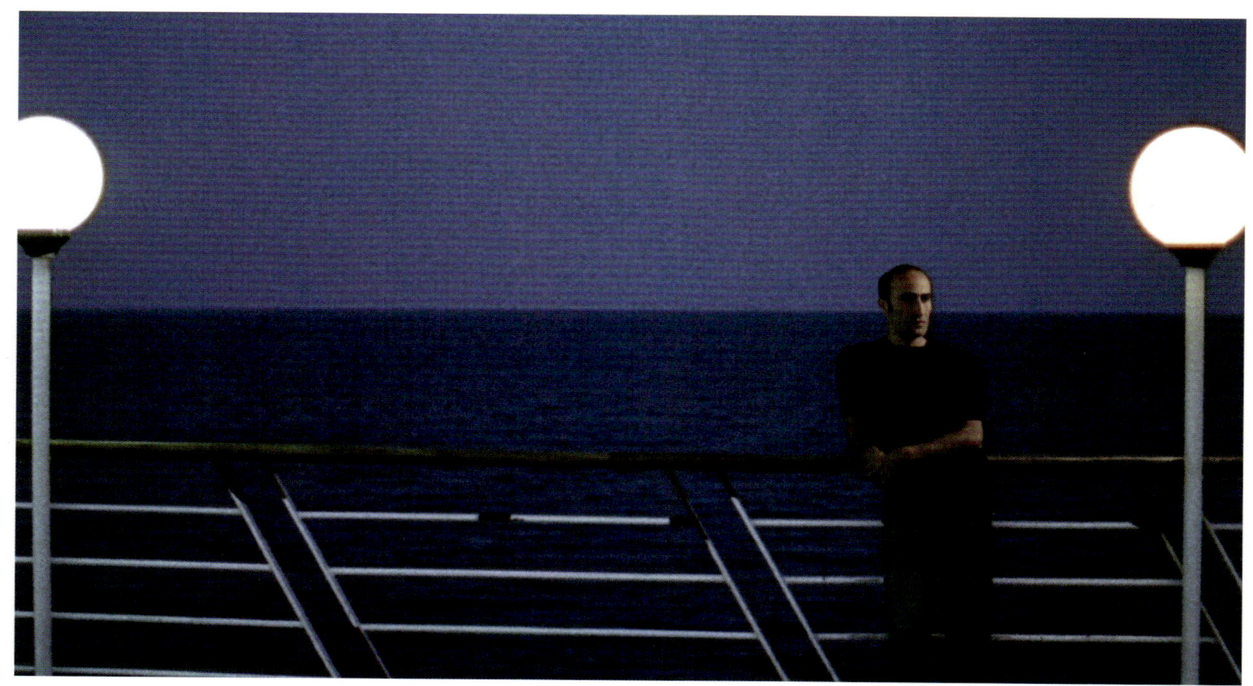

MiddleSea, *2008*
Single screen projection in 16:9
16 minutes

Another Sight, *2008*
c-print
80 x100 cm

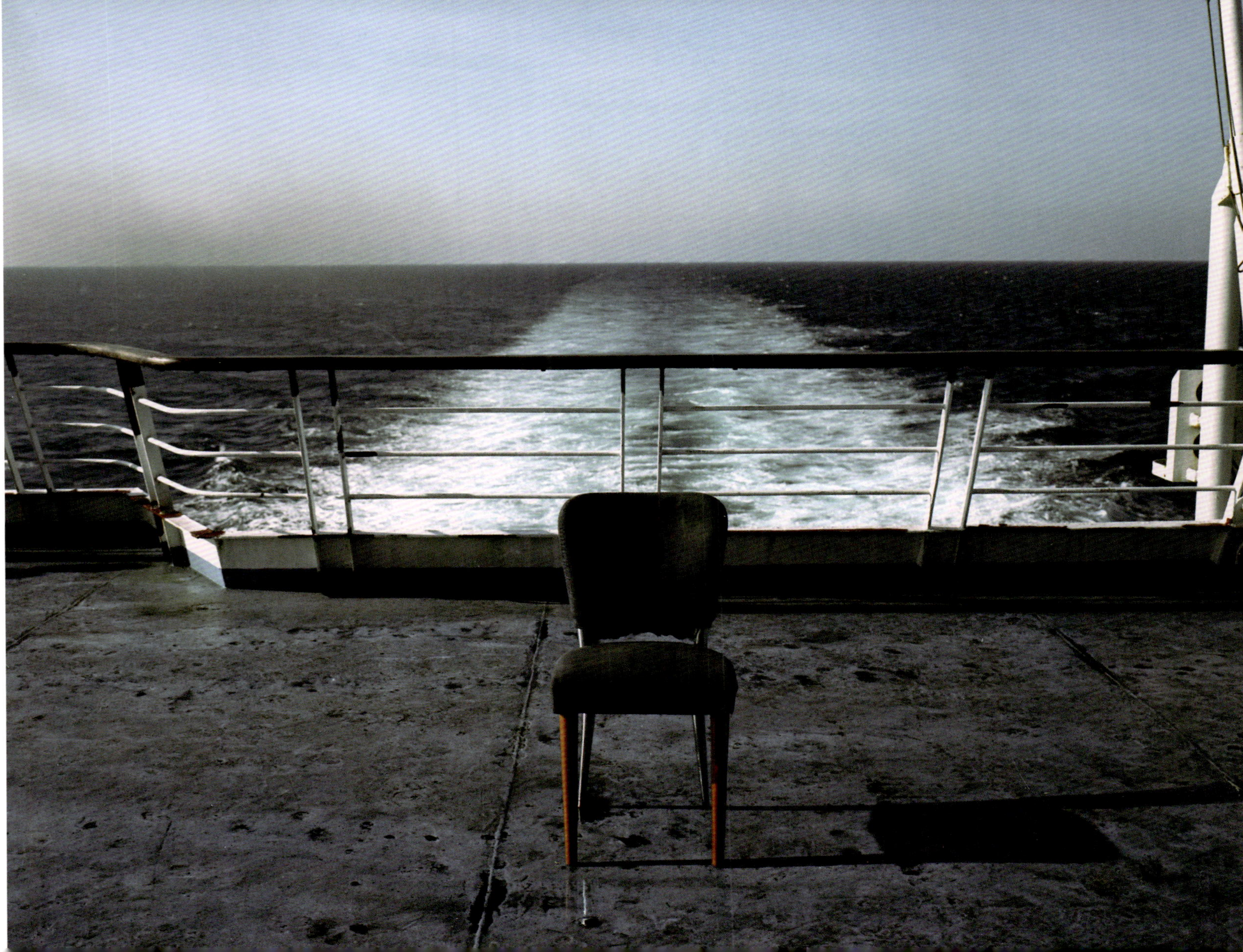

While these works explore the crumbling French architecture the still photographs *Transitional Landscape* and *Escaping the Land* document the social decay faced by local residents, disenchanted young men in particular, often dreaming of escaping across the sea to Europe.

In *Transitional Landscape*, a man is seated before the immense, mist-shrouded sea, contemplating the horizon line filled with ships in transit or awaiting permission to cross.

In *Escaping the Land*, small silhouettes of men appear to connect the sky to the beach. Subtle but intricate narratives unfold through these anonymous figures who walk, watch and wait along the shoreline, echoing the still ships.

A further reality is also explored: how individuals are directly and radically affected by social, political and environmental challenges.

The images can be seen as full of atmosphere, even poetic, but they suggest the longing of disillusioned young men, hoping to escape across the water.

In 2007, I shot *MiddleSea*, a sequel to *Saphir* that continues to explore themes of location, transition and mobility whilst further developing the poetic and cinematic narrative.

The video charts a journey by boat, between Algiers and Marseilles, an archetypal, timeless passage between two places.

Mesmerised, one can enter a space in between, transfixed by the patterns of the waves, the never-ending plumes of spray, the immense horizon. One lone passenger stares out to sea, watching, waiting. We are drawn into the narrative. Time passes, memory and imagination mix. He smokes, he drinks, dream-like he paces the deck. As one can enter the final frames, an unknown port is sighted, ropes tense and metal grinds.

MiddleSea evokes a journey taken by generations and exists in-between countries, peoples, seas and moods. It embodies all the departures, all the arrivals, and all the journeys.

A single screen installation, shot on Super 16mm colour film, each frame is hauntingly aestheticised with an audio-scape combining location sound and composed sound, created by the sound artist and performer Mikhail Karikis,

I have also produced a connected series of large photographs *Another Side* which turn the ship's mundane machinery into enticing compositions of texture and depth of field.

In the photographic triptych *A View To Sea*, the quay of an anonymous port becomes the dynamic diagonals of a Constructivist arrangement.

The vivid and graphic images illustrate details of ferries and ports, their architecture and inhabitants. Some of the images have great beauty yet they are evocative of uncertainty, disorientation and unfamiliarity.

Over the last 3 years, I have challenged myself to create new forms of both still and moving images. Working on large-scale projects involving performers, crewmembers and a producer I have achieved high quality productions. Both poetic and subtle, the works create a distance between personal, political and historical. However, it remains relevant to the ongoing local, national and international debates on globalisation.

While the issues of mobility remain central to my practice, I have, in the projects *Shipwreck: the death of a journey* (2008), expanded

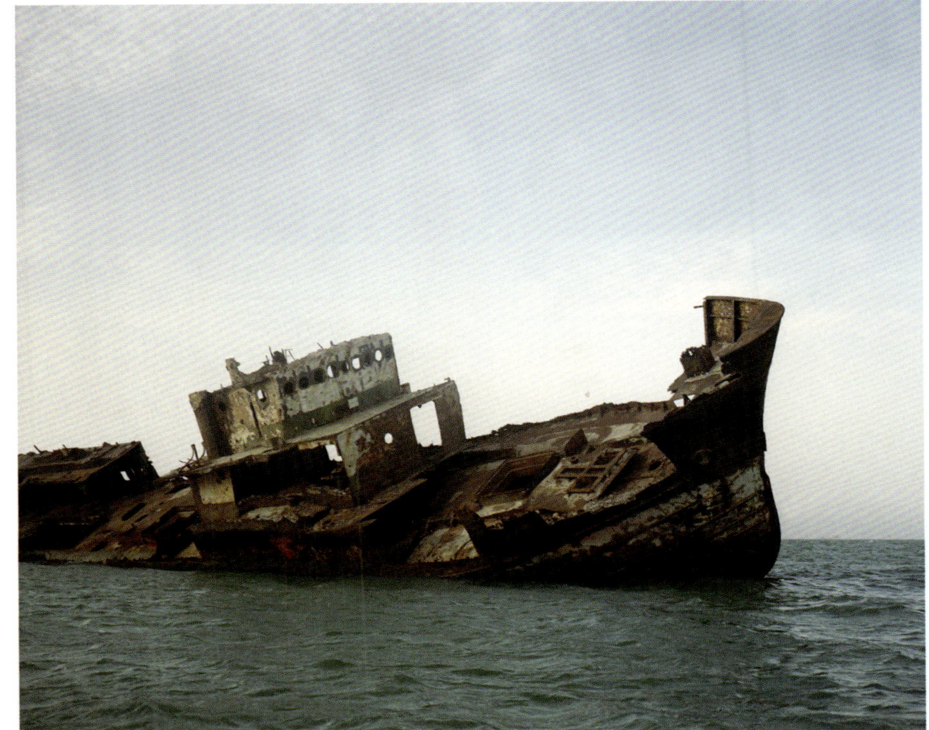

The Death of a Journey, *2008*
c-print
120 x 100 cm

The Lovers, *2008*
(next left hand page)
c-print
120 x 100 cm

Shattered Carcasses, *2008*
10 light boxes
Each light box 90 x120 cm
(next right hand page)

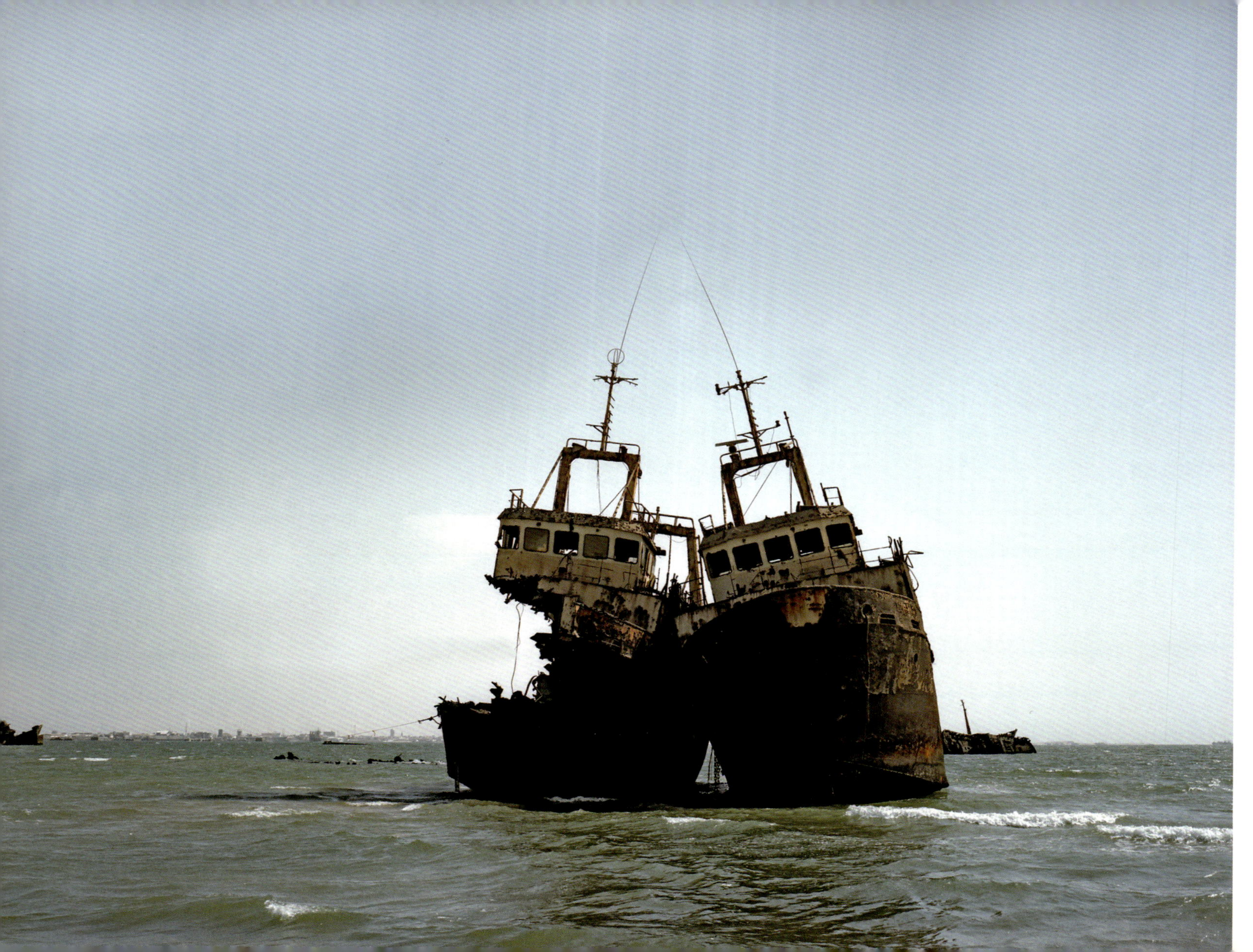

my work from the specificity of Algeria and France to include other countries because I recognise the international relevance of these themes.

My most recent project is set in Mauritania. Shot a few kilometers away from Nouadhibou, the series of photographs and light boxes installation *Shipwreck: the death of a journey* (2008) shows a darker side of the idea of transit. Like Algiers, Nouadhibou is marked by the dream of emigration. Arriving from all over Sub-Saharan Africa, people, mainly men, gather there hoping to eventually board ship for the Canary Islands.

Nouadhibou is the location for one of West Africa's most famous scrap yards for boats and ships. It is one of the few places in the world where old vessels can be dumped without first being dismantled.

Caught between sand and sea, the wrecks lie like huge rusted skeletons, sometimes vomiting their unwanted goods onto the shore. On the beach, we find hundreds of fish that have been poisoned by the noxious waters, highlighting the scale of the ecological catastrophe.

Some of the shipwrecks are leaning over and partially destroyed by water. There is a poignancy to the vision of these boats, symbols of a globalised economic system, which are destined to end their lives on these lost and ignored beaches. The photographic series is an evocation of the opposite trajectory to the migrants who leave the Mauritanians coast for the Canaries Island. Some of them fail to get away whereas others disappear at sea. Unlike the migrants, these boats depart from Europe and Asia to disembark in Mauritania.

In *Re-usable Space*, two large photographs show containers brought

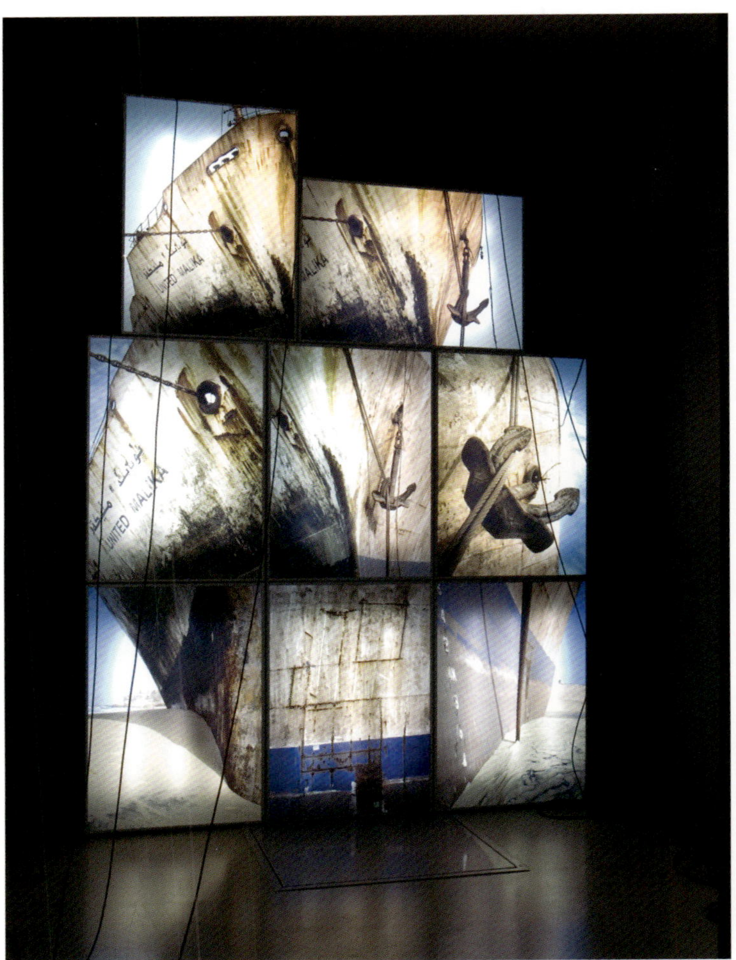

back to land and emptied only to be reused as a precarious shelter.

In *Shattered Carcasses*, several light-boxes of a fragmented boat are piled up creating a luminous sculptural installation. The electric cables of the boxes are apparent and merge with the ropes of the boat. Two additional boxes join them at the foot of the installation, portraying a pile of rusty metal and relics of boats. This fictitious 'mise-en-scene' creates the illusion of a re-assembled boat, bringing it back to life.

While my film and video work explores diaspora, identity and the movement between borders, the early work achieved this through autobiography and story telling. I constructed a complex profile of cultural, geographical and historical legacy using both non-narrative and conventional strategies and a documentary approach.

Since 2003, my work no longer centers on the family and, my role as observer is more removed, it is less narrative and spatially more expansive. I use the sea as a metaphor to explore cultural crossovers, the geo-political area as a continual interweaving of cultural roots and of historical routes. The sea becomes an intricate space of encounters, currents and continual transit: a site of ancient civilisation as well as contemporary tourism and migration.

Exploring a finely tuned visual aesthetic with landscape imagery and poetry, I am expanding the theme of displacement outside of the sometimes narrowing framework of identity and diaspora. This opens the reading of the work toward a more universal interpretation.

JEREMY DIGGLE

Fragmentary glimpses of omniana (everything)
transcribed from the performance narrative

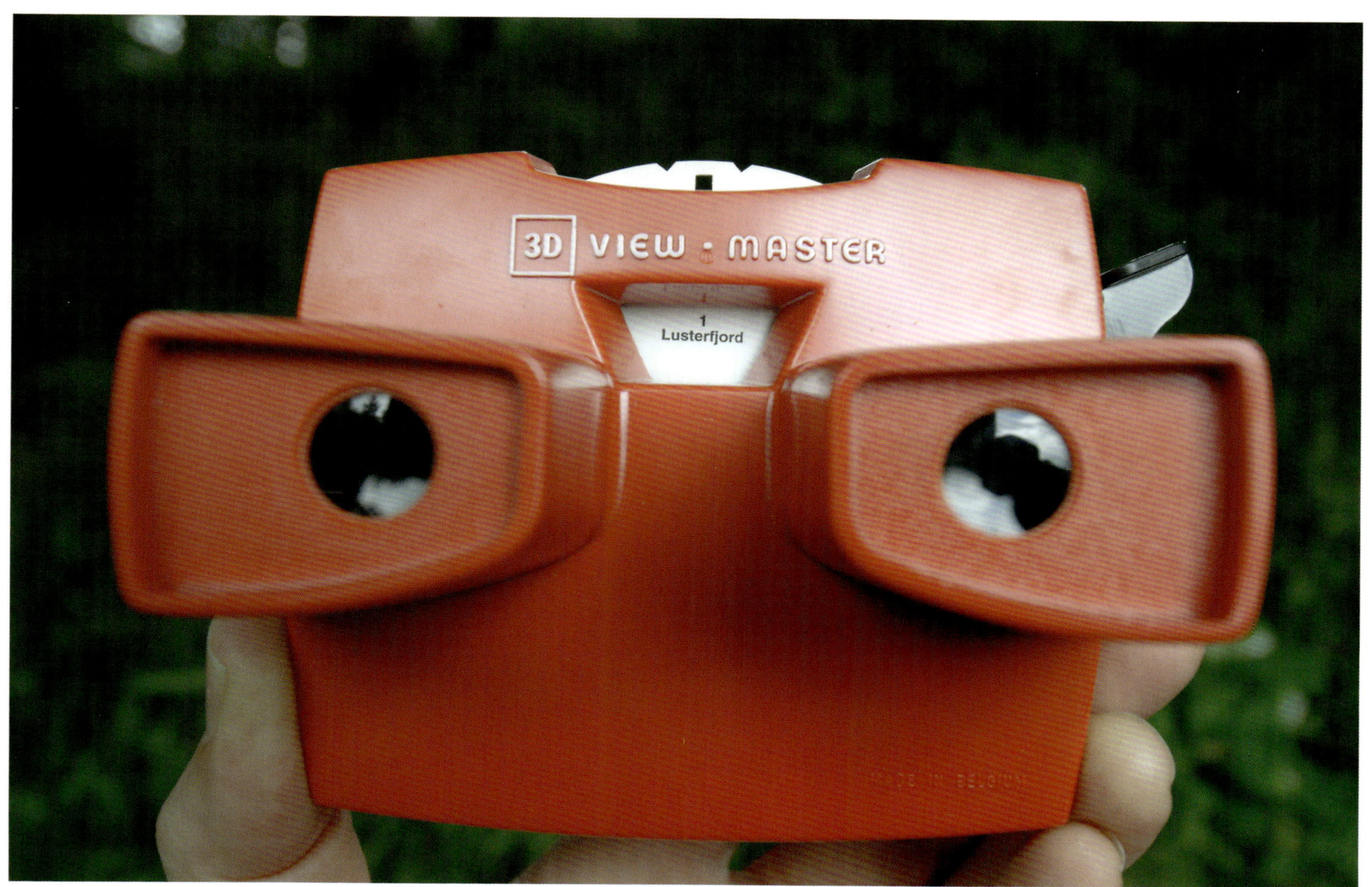

 Jeremy Diggle

Omniana (fragments of everything) an exploration of identity and meaning encapsulated in the narrative of glimpsed revelations.

There is a curious relationship between a vehicle and a fragment. A vehicle is both instrument and mien. A fragment opens the mind to what is demonstrable and possible. Vehicle recalls what gives it meaning. Be it Henry Ford's Model T, Martin Heidegger's jug, Marcel Duchamp's snow shovel, or San Gennaro's relic, the vehicle is an instrument that belongs to a wider performance of need, meaning, beauty, truth and history. A fragment implies a lost origin that leaves space for conjecture — and ultimately belief — in the demonstrability (and 'demonstrativity') of human performance. As this performance is demonstrative and demonstrable — it shows something to someone, but it is also there to be seen as something by someone. In this respect it is also unavoidable. One cannot do without its possibility.
Professor John Baldacchino, Columbia University, NY.
(Collaborator and writer on the work of Jeremy Diggle)

Viewmaster

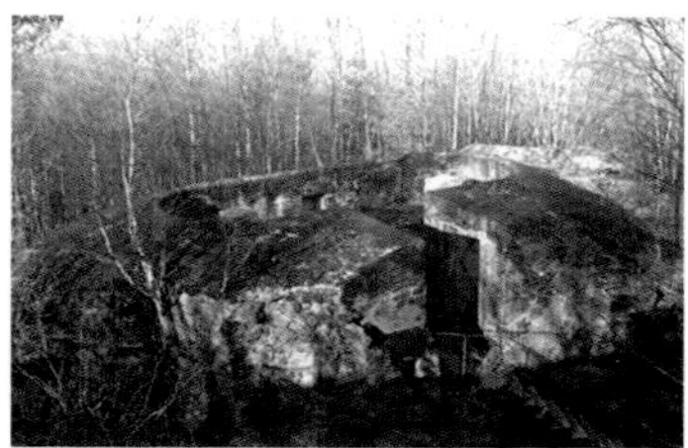

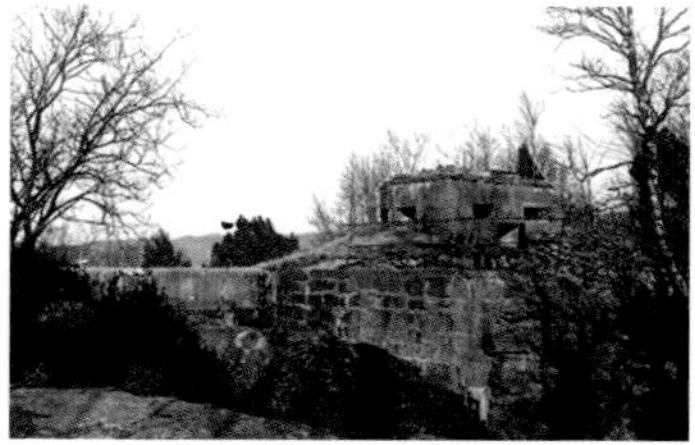

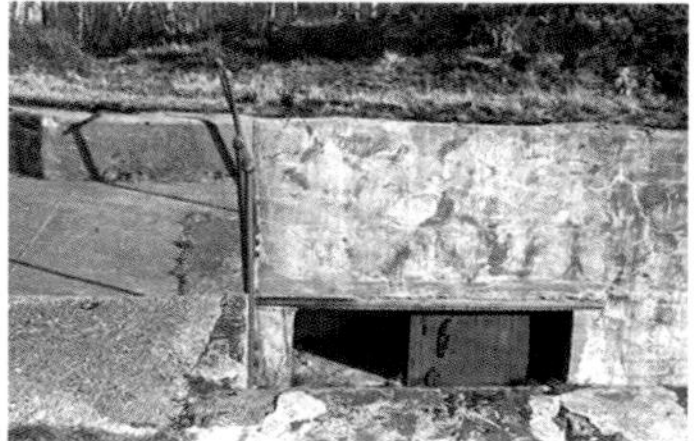

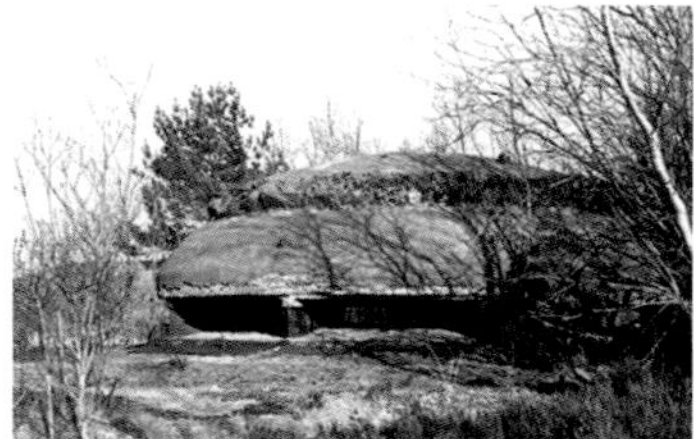

I'm going to take a risk.
Two parts,
no explanation.
It's what it is.

And there's a box.
So! Two artists, Daniel Liebens and Jacob Schokking set out on a Norwegian journey in 1992. They would end up somewhere that I would not. I would have travelled with them had it not been for being recalled to England for a couple of days on urgent business. Daniel and Jacob travelled as planned and ended up in Skjolden at the end of Lusterfjord. When I returned to Norway, to the small Wooden-house at number 4 Nagelgaden in Bergen where we were based, I waited for them to come back. On their return they brought with them stories and a gift, a fragment of a hut. Later Daniel and Jacob would publish a box set of 3D view master stereo images from this journey. [1] It is these view master slides that I will use today as my guide on this journey to somewhere.

Part 1

Jeremy is speaking to the audience whilst looking into a Viewmaster 3D viewer

What I'm looking at is a little red lighthouse; beside it are a telegraph pole and a large fjord-lake. The lighthouse is only about 2 metres tall but it's on top of a very large granite outcrop. Behind the lighthouse is a bush, beyond the bush is the lake lying absolutely calm. The surface of the lake is disturbed by the wind and there's a dark channel running through the centre of the lake where it must be absolutely calm, because the rest of the lake is reflecting the sky, which is a kind of white-ish grey. In the far distance is a fell, in the near distance to the left is another fell with trees on it and down at the very corner of the fjord to the left behind the bush are some houses and this is the departure point above the pier on the Sognefjord which lies about 140 kilometres north from Bergen on the west coast of Norway. I'm now walking along a small road and on the left hand side are some flowers, they're foxgloves, on the right hand side, on the curve, on the edge of the grass is a ditch with stinging nettles, to the left there is a white dotted line and here's a Volvo just passing. Directly in front of me is a road sign that reads Skjolden. It's a blue sign, about 2 metres high and it says '1 kilometre, Skjolden'. There's a square camp site symbol and also there's a crossed fork and spoon, there's a bed and a hut with a tree beside it and the symbols of a camping ground, 1 kilometre up the road. Just beyond the road sign is a long telegraph pole. It is densely wooded and to the left hand side are evergreens and to the right-hand side here and there are broad leaf trees, probably Birch.

I'm now stood on the prow of a hill somewhere else on Sognefjord looking down across some very large wooden houses, a couple of old Volvos parked up. It could be a guest house, probably an old farm. Beside it is a yellow wooden building, with a corrugated roof, behind

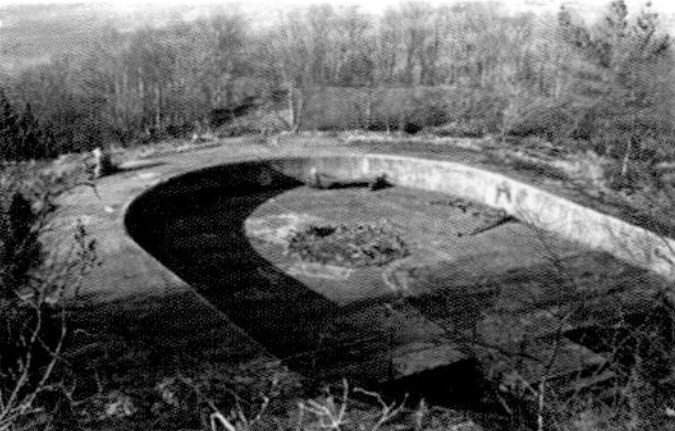

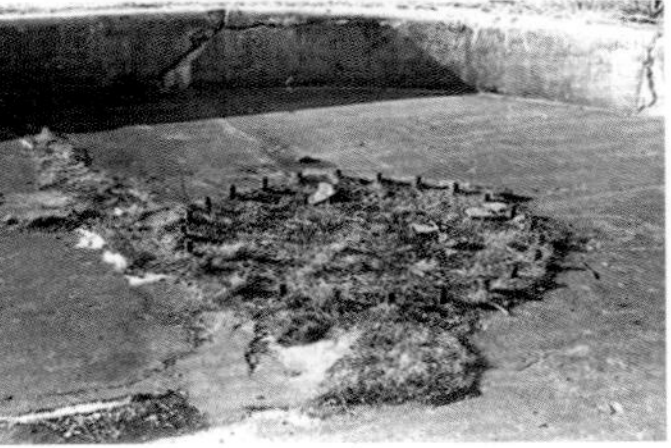

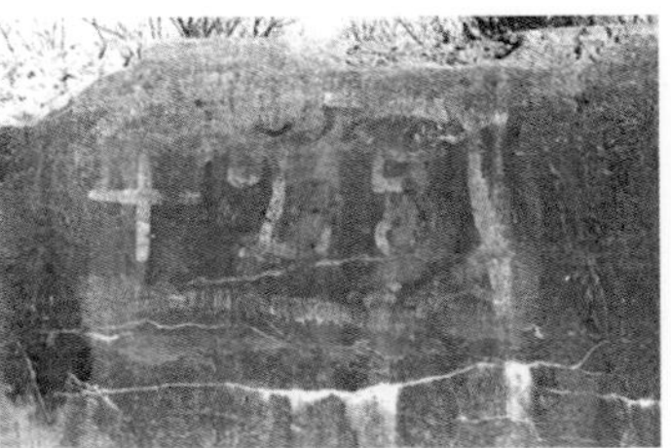

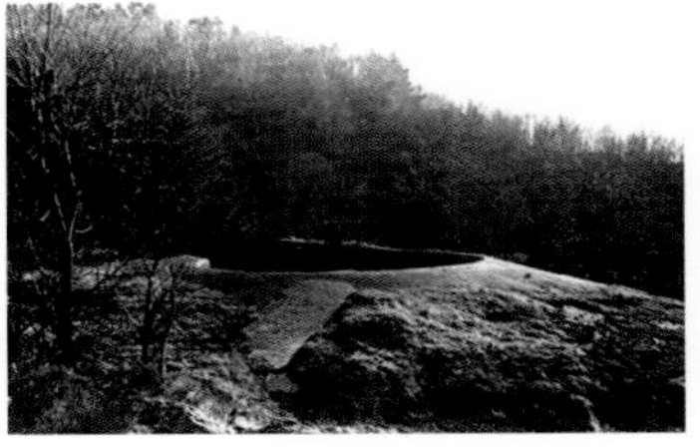

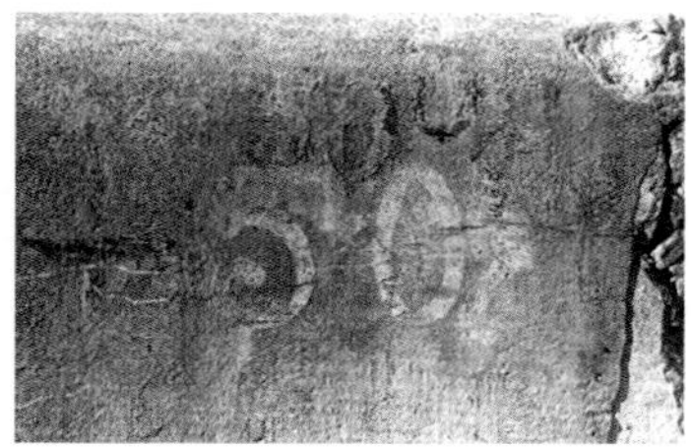

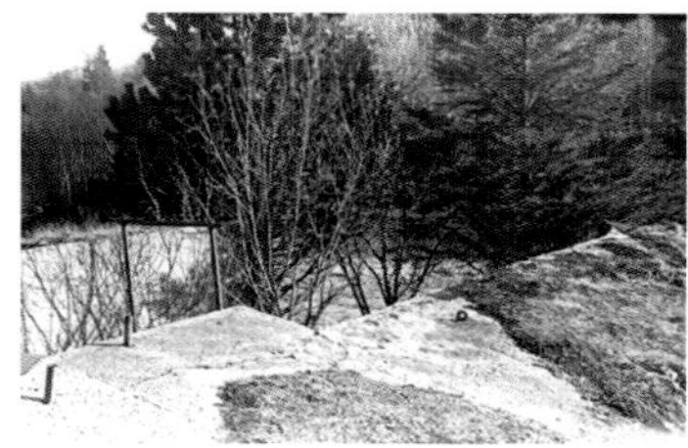

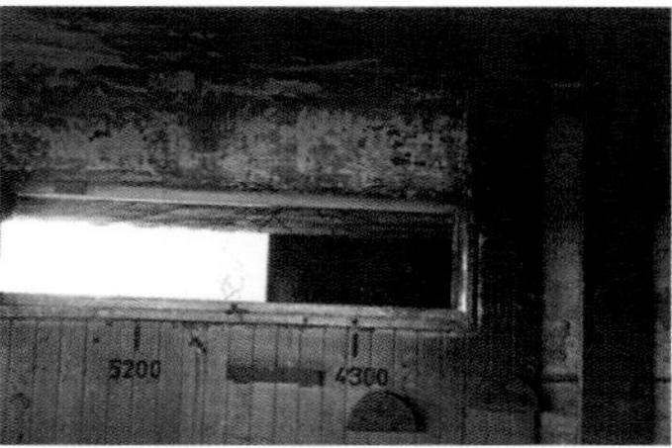

it some trees and some rusty roofs. Looking down over the top of the large buildings, over their chimneys is the lake. On the far side of the lake is a hillside rising to the right with shadows cast by the clouds above. To the left hand side of the lake is another fell rising directly and very steeply out of the water. And, in the far distance, yet another fell. It's obviously very early in the morning, it's sunny and below… running from this point where I stand, down the hill to the back of the houses is a very tall, very thick pasture of grass.

Putting the viewer down: - an aside…

I understand this landscape only by these words, not through memory, not through actual lived experience, but by words coming into being as I look through this viewer. It (the landscape) has no other meaning for me than that which is formed by descriptive words giving shape to an idea.

…And if you will allow me a small indulgence, by way of marking the start of this journey, I'm going to give a quick toast in a language that is now dead, that doesn't exist anymore, it's been sleeping for a thousand years, dormant within our modern English, a thousand year old North Sea language, an utterance from the first lines of the prologue to the Beowulf.

> **H**wæt! We Gardena   in geardagum,
> _eodcyninga,   _rym gefrunon,
> hu _a æ_elingas   ellen fremedon.

The emphasis here is upon "**H**wæt!"

"**H**wæt" is sometimes translated as "attend". There are a number of interpretations but essentially it is a word that has no precise translation. As an example you could liken it to one of those great German words, which we've incorporated into contemporary English, like "angst", for which there is no precise English equivalent. "**H**wæt"…the very sound of it, challenges you to attend, bare witness, listen, gather, a perfect beginning word. For instance in the recent translation of the Beowulf, by Seamus Heaney, he has translated "**H**wæt" to be the word "So", but only Seamus Heaney can say the word "So" in such a way as to be a call to attention, a beginning, and yet carry the sense of a continued moment as if a story or anecdote, having been told, is about to be superseded by a far grander narrative… So! You had better listen.

"Attend", an invitation to pay attention, nothing will happen unless you pay attention, this is the beginning of the story."

Putting the viewer back to his eyes: -

I'm down at the water's edge. This fjord is not an entirely enclosed lake, the water is running very fast in front of me. You can tell by the disturbance that it obviously has a deep river current running beneath the still waters, there's a maelstrom…another of those words that we've only recently acquired into everyday English language.

It's obviously extremely dangerous to cross this water. It must be about 100 metres across and on the other side are fishing cottages. What I recognise is that I'm now stood on the opposite side to where

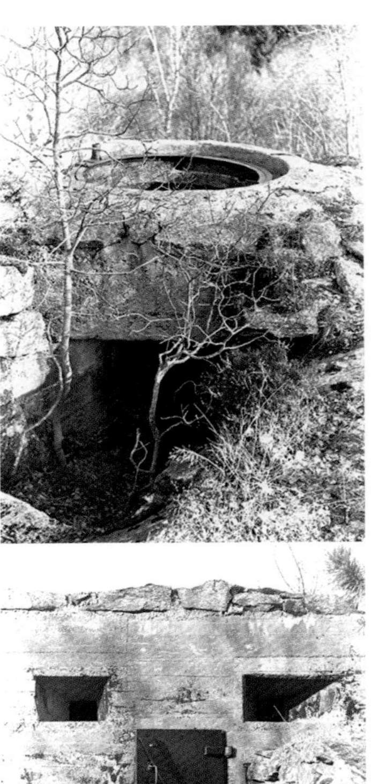

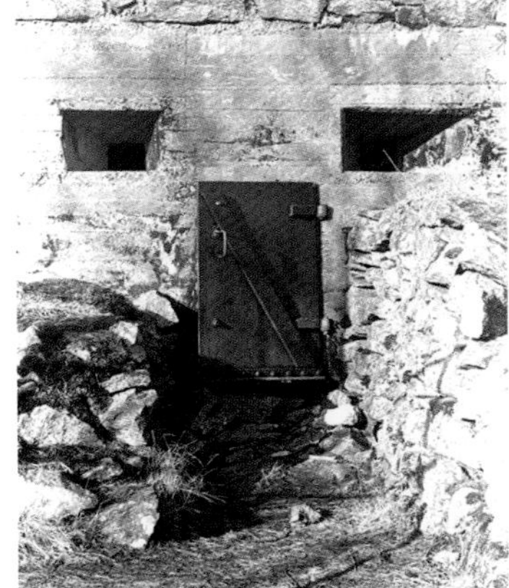

I last described. The very large house in the distance is the house that I was stood behind on the top of the crest of a hill looking down over the thick pasture grass. Looking back this way, there is an extremely large fell rising straight out behind a bluff where I was stood before which is capped by trees. It rises so steeply there is no way you could judge where the top of it would end. The large fishing cottage to my left is brilliant white in the sunshine as are all these buildings. This is the settlement of Skjolden, which has about 160 people in it. It's an ancient crossroads on the Sognefjord, just up from an area outside Bergen called Flam and the population has been consistently 160 for about 4 or 5 hundred years.

I think I'm going to be getting into a boat.

Putting the viewer down: - an aside…

Back in 1992 as I remember it, (this is my recollection of that occasion and memory can sometimes be false), I saw the most extraordinary thing in Bergen harbour. It was the departure of three Viking boat replicas. Although they were replicas they were in everyway authentic, they were the real-thing. Hand built in a place like the Flam Wharf beyond Aurland and Onstad, in the heart of a fjord or possibly on inlet by the coast in Iceland. They came into Bergen Harbour on May 17th, which is Norway's national day, in order to make a formal departure, to sail to America and to prove that is was possible that likes of Leif Erikson and the various Norwegian, Danish and Icelandic crews of history had the ability to navigate those boats in open seas to America.

The remarkable thing about watching from the top of a high-rise building on the waterfront in Bergen was to see them surrounded literally by a thousand other small boats. The whole of Bergen harbour appeared to be completely full of these fibreglass and wooden flotsam punctuated by dark-islands of larger naval vessels.

At precisely 4 o'clock in the afternoon there was a light breeze from the east and absolute silence. The three Viking boats, sails unfurled, let loose their moorings ever so slowly. Everything else in the harbour then moved almost imperceptibly to the left and parted, leaving just one dark stream of water. The three boats sailed out through the harbour, through the armada of small craft. The sirens of the naval boats sounded, a submarine appeared, and all the flotsam of small boats turned and followed them out to the open sea. It was the most extraordinary scene.

Putting the viewer back to his eyes: -

What I'm looking at now is a large wooden hut. In the foreground in the long grass are roof tiles, those zigzagged, curly, brick red roof tiles. Beyond that is a small line of very young Birch trees, very, very thin and a tiny fir tree and over to my left hand side some pieces of wood and debris of building and a role of large agricultural chicken wire. The sun is shining down and it's very dappled grass. Beyond that little line, filling three-quarters of this picture that I'm looking at, is this white grey wooden hut three storeys high, it's got a basement and then it's got 2 storeys with steep leaning roof which is tiled in grey, I can't quite understand why there are all these red roofing tiles, for this is a grey roofed classic Norwegian wood building. A large pile of freshly chopped wood is outside a small extension to the back of the house and over to the left a large area of concrete with tarpaulin and if I look very carefully by the drainpipe there's a small blue plaque.

I'm now on the road again. I'm looking this way into the sunshine. An extremely dark line of trees to my left; I'm at the edge of a bridge!

There's a red caution sign… red almost barbershop red, white, red, white… stood about a metre tall on a small pole with a concrete base, by the white dotted line that runs along the side of the bridge. I'm on tarmac by the edge of the bridge and the water's running under it and there's a road sign beyond the bridge which I can't read. No matter how hard I try I can't read it and behind which are some very tall, elegant fir trees and then the bright sunlit, tree-clad fell and another electric pylon. Sun across the bridge, silence, I don't think a car's come through here for several hours.

Putting the viewer down: - an aside…

At this moment I genuinely don't know where I am going, just following in the tracks of my two friends.

Putting the viewer back to his eyes: -

We're in a boat. A rowing boat and I'm sat at the back of the boat. Jacob has one oar to the right and Daniel has an oar to the left. The oar is above the water. The water is chromium-oxide green, a sort of milky, milk'blue green. There is a triangle of light. The water is unbroken. The oar sits quarter of a metre above. It's a very old oar, very long, the full horizon of the picture. Above that, right through the centre of the picture is a pure glass-cut line on the water where the water meets a rising fell.

Grey, green, brown, granite, with some trees, a cave and to the right a landing point brightly lit, and behind that a very large hill covered in trees and there is a beautiful blue sky. We're obviously heading in the direction of the triangle of light on the other side. It looks like Austria.

We're now in the middle of the lake and I'm standing up and I can see through the binoculars a platform, a platform of very large, granite bricks, on top of a granite cliff face. It must be 100 metres above the waterline. To the right is a flagpole. There's no wind but there is a flag on it. It's in red and white, an Austrian flag, surrounded by Birch trees which look like blood vessels sticking up out of the ground, drained of blood which has gone down into the granite and down into the lake… The blue sky above, one large dark tree on the fore shore.

At this point we are arriving at what appears to be a sort of Robinson-Crusoe-like platform of white sand and clear azure blue water, where you can see the sand reflecting beneath it. There's a bush, rhododendrons, oak, a very rare species in Norway. Thickets of Birch and we're very close to a large lump of granite here. It looks like we're on the edge of some exotic swimming pool really. We're about to make landfall and in front of me in the centre of the picture through the gap in the trees is a pathway, where very few people have walked. You can tell it's a pathway, there's a gap, a small dark gap in the trees with

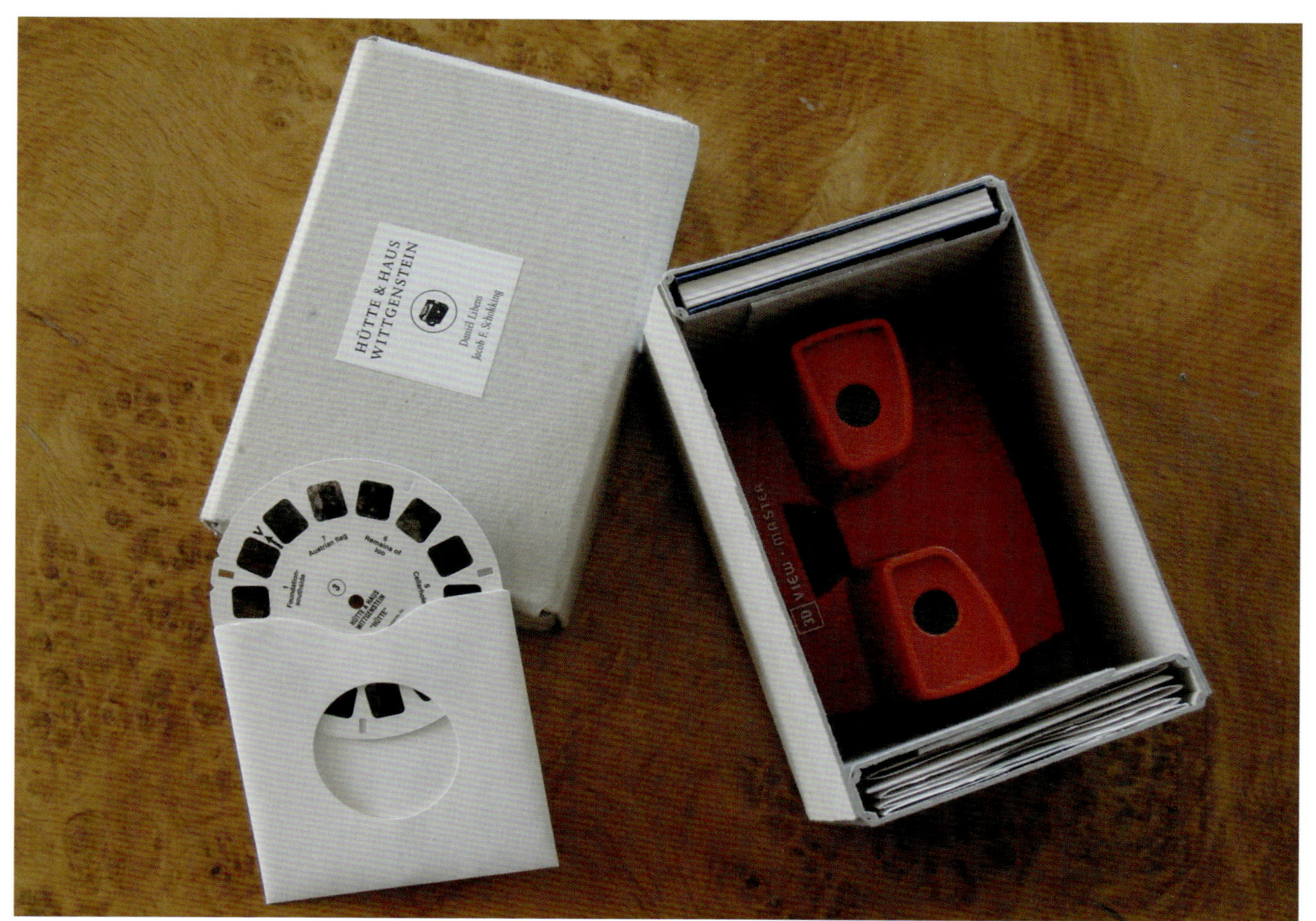

HÜTTE & HAUS
WITTGENSTEIN
Danid Libens
Jacob F. Schokking
3D VIEW-MASTER

smaller evergreens growing and one fine line of stinging nettles, which obviously follows the path of the last person who walked through.

…Very strong sunlight dappling through….

We make landfall and the gap opens up as we walk up through the trees but the rocks are thickly covered in wet, sphagnum moss. Small Beech is growing here and grass, in fact these are all Beech trees and through the gap is a small bluff of rock and a ladder and what looks like a well worn footpath that has been carved at some point in the past but has been worn down so it looks like it's has always been there, but it has obviously been cut into the granite face. And sticking out of that rock is a multitude of young sapling trees. No evergreens here. Some old tin can. And over here evidence of someone was having had a bonfire last spring? Last autumn? A year old bonfire and some Fox Gloves.

It's a very monotonous landscape, very dense but now we are getting to a very well worn brick, heavily overgrown footpath, with a dangerous stone surface. It's the sort of stone where you can imagine if you get it wrong you're going to break your ankle and you're not going to get any further up. There's a piece of graffiti on the left hand side…

…But it's a very easy walk up here. It's a tourist path and we're very close to the base of that large granite bluff. Small cave, but it's not deep, just an indentation and a beautiful birch tree, white and grey.

We're now right on the edge of a precipice. We have to go round this large rock fall. Someone has graffitied in red 'Fuck'. But the footpath winds round, it's almost like a medieval church stairwell going up, it's turning, you could be in a castle but you're not. Beyond it is a large, grey cliff face that goes down to the lake below. There's a large, metal pole sticking out in the distance catching the light. Beyond that is a bird, the first wildlife I've seen. There's a bird holding station. It's some kind of small falcon. Beyond which are a line of trees again hanging precariously on this cliff face.

I've walked all the way up the path and now I'm looking down onto this extraordinary turquoise blue lake but at the angle I'm looking down I can see reflected the fell on the cliff face beyond and the trees but I'm looking at almost three-quarters of a fjord of turquoise water but in front of that is a piece of scaffolding. A scaffolding pole, upturned angular u-form, with a hook and beyond that some small trees, some parsleys and cow parsley and an incredibly steep granite slope with bleached grass and a deep, deep fall.

We are **somewhere** now. We're at the platform which is a foundation, huge pieces of carved granite rock foundation with dark shadows of the trees and beyond which again is this cliff face of granite but it is entirely surrounded by small birch.

It's a large square foundation with plants standing up inside it. It's very wet. It barely sticks out of the ground like part of an archaeological dig, but it's there. It's ready to take a new platform on top. There's a deep hole, it's obviously a cellar hole. The sphagnum moss is rotting. There are dry patches and extremely wet patches. There are fresh footprints probably Jacob Schokking's, the odd brick, but nothing else.

We're now looking out across the lake, deep, deep, lake in the far distance. A large corner of platform in front of me, with the view deep down and a tree on the right with Sun coming across the incredibly

Viewmaster box set
(previous left hand page)

Wittgenstein's hut

88 Jeremy Diggle

sturdily built platform. This is a late nineteenth century or maybe early twentieth century platform. In the far distance though are some agricultural fields, there's a field of cows. It must be a kilometre away. Very small trees line it, there's a very slight slope. A field of cows and a farm house, and the wind is just catching the lake from the left.

We're now in front of a steep, 2 metre tall front-face of the platform. There's a hole in front of the platform that juts out with a water pipe and you can see that from the platform here, a metre out and then it drops absolutely sheer down to the lake below. Beyond which is a sheer face of cliff because it drops away again on the right hand side and there's a gap down to the lake and the cliff beyond.

I'm now stood right in the middle of the platform and there's a deep hole with old iron and rubber junk and a plant growing out of it. To the back of the platform, again surrounded by new birch, is a hole and some wood. It's got pieces of wood, small, small fragments of wood. This is the toilet, the outside loo, the only fragments of wood that are left from this hut.

Jacob Shocking is kneeling down and picking a fragment from the hole. He's putting it in a grey box. He's sniffing it. The sun is shining. He's got the Austrian flag in his hands.

End of Part 1

Jeremy is holding a fragment of aged grey wood

"I have a fragment of Wittgenstein's hut. In my eyes that's about as good as it gets for a secular relic.

I guess you could test if for DNA.

I know of only 3 other fragments, I've got one, and I believe Daniel's got one and Jacob's got one. The rest are at the site of the relic, the hut above the fjord, a kind of *'site of special philosophical interest'* …

So, this presentation, the *telling*, a journey to somewhere, was a kind of humble attempt to demonstrate in practice my understanding of a fragment of the philosophy of Wittgenstein. This understanding can be paraphrased as "nothing exists as thoughts or ideas, all is framed in the moment, in language this is how things are."

So, this is the first time through *telling*, that I've gone on the journey to see Wittgenstein's hut. Originally when I had intended to travel with my two friends up to Skjolden I had had to travel back to England and by the time I got back to the house in Bergen they had already been. This is the *telling* of a journey never taken.

(Looking at the fragment of wood in his hands)

So, I wasn't there when this relic was removed.
It was a gift

And it would not matter if this relic wasn't what it is reported to be either, because I believe it is authentic. I know it is what it is and it is the knowledge of that which is important… that is the point.

The interesting thing for me, in this moment, is to experience someone else's view of the landscape and to share their binocular recording of that landscape through a telling of a journey to somewhere that I have never been. To see through their fixed view, no movement, pre-selected, virtual and to understand something. Obviously I can't smell it, I can't taste it and I have not crossed the water or climbed the hills with the ache in my legs. However, I can travel with them there having read some of Wittgenstein books and holding this relic…

Taking the fragment of Wittgenstein's hut and placing it beneath his nose Jeremy makes an allusion to reliquary "fragments of the true cross"

(Joking)… As a result I feel a little bit closer to Wittgenstein, although I must say I feel even closer to Wittgenstein when I inhale…

Of course this fragment could be entirely a fiction but then I suspect Wittgenstein's Norway has certainly been fictionalised to.

"Bugger off! Get your cows out the way I'm trying to think!" comes to mind when imagining Ludwig's concentrated stare into the far distance.

This is surely one of the great fictions about Wittgenstein the hermit. In fact he had people round him, he entertained them and could apparently be convivial. The only thing that he would apparently insist upon would be, not to speak to you until he had finished his work.

Part Two

A screening of a series of images and text with audio track. (A multimedia reconstruction of the artists book 'Norway Time 3 Additions'.)

This slide show and other related information is available for view at: www.norwayti.me.uk

Conversationally and by way of setting a context (holding the fragment of wood): -

I wanted to show this work as an example of another particular experience of landscape and to place the first 'telling' within a context of another particular journey, one that I under took long ago in 1975. This series of photographs, the book, record an experience of time and place in the Norwegian landscape. The photographs, the book, eventually led to a performative-action and the graffiti work, which I carried out at the site of a WW2 German bunker above the coastal entrance to Bergen harbour. The work was very much a youthful and emotional response to a particular place and circumstance, with a resulting argument encapsulated within the book-work, that is, simply, you can't vandalise Nazi architecture. That early personal discovery however came about through a journey to a place on a map, a city on the coast and the discovery of a 'somewhere' the likes of which I had never experienced before.

I first went to Norway on a quest to find the *Beowulf*, to undertake a journey of self-discovery, a search for the hero within. I didn't find that hero, but I did discover an evocative landscape, both internal and external. The Beowulf was the text I carried with me when I set off for those foreign shores on a boat from Newcastle. It was a kind of divinational map of where I wanted to go. I would use it as an interpretive tool a kind of 'metaphysical rough guide' to the landscape.

Over the years the *Beowulf* has become so intertwined with my experience of Norway, that there is now a conflict that I have in the separation between the memory of the physical experience of being in that particular landscape, and the metaphysical euphoria of being young and on a landscape journey, that I interpreted through that particular word-hoard of the story.

I inherited automatically through the Christian tradition of my early childhood education and upbringing, an experience of going out into the landscape, especially wilderness, one that is shot through with a sense of wonder and awe for nature. A landscape full of metaphysics and empathy with a creator God, no matter how atheistic I have become through rational learning, for example through the reading and interpretation of the expulsion of metaphysics by someone like Wittgenstein. I'm sure that I probably fail to understand much of Wittgenstein, but the irony, even if I misunderstand completely, amuses me anyway, of the great Austrian who has to go into the wilderness to perch in a hut, above a fjord, in order to really focus down on the expulsion of metaphysics from the mind, so as to free and to liberate thought and to understand that you bring things into being through language at the moment you think them.

So, everything happens in real time. I now think the experience of walking out in nature is like this. It's not predetermined; you can't really go out there with a pre-thought of what you are going to experience, although at one level we always do, as we have this internal communicator that's always conversing within ourselves. To experience the landscape I now think you have to get the sequence right, making sure that the internal communicator isn't telling you what to see, but what you are seeing.

(Looking at the fragment of wood in his hands)

Although it's a fragment, this is not the myth of the hut, this is the hut.

What I have tried to set out to do here, albeit probably relatively unsuccessfully, is to say that this fragment (a true relic), extracted from a "somewhere", represents a very particular intellectual landscape, the one which I now inhabit. By way of contrast I have shown another landscape, 'somewhere' from another point of view, from another position in time and place shaped by another and different worldview.

In conclusion

When I was a First Year art student at St Martins School of art, we had a Korean professor of painting come to visit. He took a liking to me because I was exploring landscape and figurative work with which he felt he could engage. I was painting using traditional received notions of Renaissance perspective. This professor sat me down one day and tried to explain to me, that when interpreting the landscape, traditional Renaissance perspective views of the landscape can be a trap, because what they imply is that somewhere out there is a 'beautiful view'. This notion of a perspective view of the landscape leads you to go out into the landscape and paint the beautiful view. You put a rectangle around it, you take it away and ultimately you trade it. It becomes an object of material exchange. You, as *'genius'*, extract this beautiful view for your own esteem, to either own it or trade it. The beautiful view, as represented through the convention of perspective, is captured nature. The argument, he put forward, followed that you have seen 'somewhere' over there and you have captured everything that radiates from that point, to which all lines appear to recede into the distance, into the centre of your rectangle. However you have composed the beautiful view from a single point of view, a point of view that lacks knowledge. The professor explained that in another tradition you would go into the landscape and you would find a beautiful view and this would be somewhere to get to. So you would then have to travel from here, the point where you perceive the beautiful view, to there, the point of knowledge. On that journey through the landscape you record the experience and when you get 'somewhere'… *that is the beautiful view.* Everything that is the experience of the landscape, between where you saw where you wanted to go and to where you have arrived, is the embodiment of the landscape. In essence a complete reversal of traditional perspective, because from that point of view of Renaissance perspective, you now stand at the vanishing point, looking back to the original point of perception, the lines of radiation are reversed. If you just stand and look out at the view you have no experience of it. The 'somewhere' is actually over there. If you look back, you already know something. That something has stuck with me, the idea that you are nowhere until you've been somewhere. So there was a kind of relationship to that. And for me the 'somewhere' is here.

(Holding out the fragment of wood)

So, if there was a place to get to, this 'somewhere' exists in my hands. It's only real there. It's not real anywhere else, the journey to it is a journey to somewhere. The 'somewhere' is where you arrive and you extract something physical, otherwise it always remains elsewhere. A journey-away. I think it becomes somewhere at the point of determination, where you say, this is 'somewhere'. This is the beautiful view. This is the body of the text.

NOTES

[1] *Hutte & Haus Wittgenstein* by Libens, D & Schokking, J F. Published by Holland House 1995

LAND/WATER AND THE VISUAL ARTS

The core priority of the LAND/WATER research group is support for the development of individual creative and critical practices. As artists, curators and writers we generate original objects and messages that question, reconsider and renew the nature and use of visual language. These works contribute both to contemporary academic debates within artistic and curatorial practices, and to understanding within related areas of experience and knowledge. Our approach is also interdisciplinary and collaborative. Through exhibitions, books and installations we establish a direct dialogue with the public, often in new and unusual locations and environments. Central concerns include: sustainability; representation of change; journey, place and visual practice; West Country and regional specificity. There is particular focus on coast as a littoral space, and interest in exploring relations between site – theme - art process - narrative.

Creative practice is now acknowleged as a field of academic research and has changed significantly as a result. Over the past decade we have established a strong base for the group through individual works, commissions, residencies, exhibitions, publications, discussions and debates and research studentships and supervision. Members of the group work internationally through research, professional practice and exhibition. Living in the South-West of Britain nonetheless crucially informs modes of research and visual perception.

The intentions of the research group are to:
- contribute to knowledge and understanding within the field of landscape studies especially in relation to landscape practices.
- foster creativity, debate and experimentation within the field.
- enhance the international academic profile of group members.
- develop collaborations both within and beyond the discipline
- promote our research to an international constituency through conferences, seminars, publications and joint projects.
- foster postgraduate taught and research opportunities within the University, which have a significant focus on landscape and environment.

Group Membership
Gursewak Aulakh (Lecturer in Architecture)
Carole Baker (Photographer; Lecturer in Photography)
Sue Blackburn (Research Fellow, Serio)
Caroline Burke (Photographer; Lecturer in Media Arts)
Christopher Cook (Artist; Reader in Painting)
Susan Derges (Artist; Research Fellow, Photography)
David Hilton (Artist; Subject Leader, Media Arts)
Andy Klunder (Artist; Subject Leader in Fine Art)
Polly Macpherson (Ceramicist; Award Leader, Designer Maker-3D Design)
Heidi Morstang (Photographer; Lecturer in Photography)
Liz Nicol (Artist/Photographer; Head of School of Art and Media)
Jem Southam (Photographer; Professor in Photography)
Simon Standing (Photographer; Subject Leader, Photography)
Steve Thorpe (Artist; Lecturer in Fine Art)
Stephen Vaughan (Photographer; Lecturer in Photography)
Liz Wells (Writer/Curator; Professor in Photographic Culture; Director, Land/Water & the Visual Arts)

Publications include:
Liz Wells and Simon Standing, *Surface*, 2005
Liz Wells and Simon Standing, *Change*, 2007
Liz Wells and Simon Standing, *Fictions*, 2008

For further information email liz.wells@plymouth.ac.uk

BIOGRAPHIES

Jeremy Diggle has established an international reputation for his use of technology and highly crafted narrative work. He has worked in holography, photography, video and multimedia. He is Professor of Fine Art and Head of the School of Fine Arts and Photography at Massey University, Wellington. Previous posts include: Associate Dean of Research (Faculty of Arts) and Professor of Fine Art at the University of Plymouth; Professor of Fine Art and Head of ELAM School of Art, The University of Auckland; and Research Professor and Head of School at Gray's School of Art, the Robert Gordon University Aberdeen, Scotland.

Tim Edgar began photographing the urban landscape when a Commercial Photographer in Bristol in the late 1980's. In 1990 he was Photographer in Residence at Whitchurch Psychiatric Hospital, Cardiff. In 1998 he completed an MA in Documentary Photography at Newport. In 2000 he moved to Swanage, Dorset. *Rookery* was published, and exhibited at The Arts Institute at Bournemouth in 2003, where he is a Senior Lecturer in Photography. *Subterrane* will be exhibited in 2008, and published with 3 other Photographers as *Locale* which continues to explore the (mis)representation of Hardy's Dorset.

Guy Moreton is an artist and Senior Lecturer in Photography at Southampton Solent University, UK. He was a guest artist in Rotterdam, Netherlands and Scottish Arts Council Fellow in Photography at Napier University, Edinburgh. His work is engaged with the cultural histories and representation of landscape and architecture in literature, art and philosophy; and has been published, exhibited and critically reviewed internationally, notably in the Whitechapel Gallery London, EAST International Norwich, the John Hansard Gallery Southampton and in *Waterlog* curated by Jeremy Millar for the Norwich Castle and the Sainsbury Centre for Visual Arts 2007. He is co-author, *Ludwig Wittgenstein There Where You Are Not,* London: Black Dog. Moreton was included in Tacita Dean and Jeremy Millar, *Place* London: Thames and Hudson, 2005.

Zineb Sedira came to London in 1986 and studied art at the Slade School of Art and the Royal College of Art. She has exhibited her work in Europe, the US and the Middle East. Amongst many, the Venice Biennale (2001), Tate Britain (2002), ICP Triennial, NY (2003), PhotoEspana, Madrid (2004), Centre Pompidou & Hayward Gallery (2005), British Art Show 06 (2006), Sharjah Biennale and the 1st Thessaloniki Biennale (2007). Selected solos at the Galerie Esma, Algiers and at the Photographers Gallery, London (2006).

Simon Standing is Subject Leader for Photography, University of Plymouth. He completed his PhD in 2000, in which he developed photography as a primary research method of enquiry investigating the relationship between design and ritual in the Anglican Church. Current research is concerned with ways in which photography represents and interprets time and change, with projects that explore ideas of the English rural idyll, and Plymouth City's regeneration. With Liz Wells and Jem Southam he was organiser of *Framing Time and Place: Repeats and Returns in Photography*, University of Plymouth photography conference, April 2009.

Harriet Tarlo is a poet and academic who lives in Holmfirth, West Yorkshire. She is a Senior Lecturer in Creative Writing at Sheffield Hallam University. Recent poetry publications include *Love/Land*, REM press, 2003; *Poems 1990-2003*, Shearsman Books, 2004 and *Nab*, Etruscan Books, 2005. Her poems about the Cumbrian coast currently appear with Jem Southam's *Clouds Descending* photographic exhibition at The Lowry Gallery, Salford, a collaboration born of the Land/Water Symposium in 2007. Tarlo's special feature on eco-poetry appears in the current issue of the journal How2 Vol 3: No 2 (http://www.asu.edu/pipercwcenter/how2journal/). She is currently co-editing a volume on British Eco-criticism with the University of Virginia Press, editing *The Ground Aslant,* an anthology of radical landscape poetry for Shearsman Press (due for publication in 2010) and preparing her latest collection for publication with the same press.

Ian Walker is Reader in the History of Photography at the University of Wales, Newport. He has written extensively about photography, making a particular study of the relationship between Documentary and Surrealism. In 2002, he published his book *City Gorged with Dreams: Surrealism and Documentary Photography in Interwar Paris* (Manchester University Press). This was followed in 2007 by *So Exotic, So Homemade: Surrealism, Englishness and Documentary Photography* (also published by MUP) and this essay is closely related to the chapter on Paul Nash. He has also published and exhibited his own photographs widely, most recently in Greece and France.

Liz Wells writes and lectures on photographic practices. She is editor of *The Photography Reader*, 2003 and of *Photography: A Critical Introduction*, 2009, 4th ed.; also co-editor of *photographies*, Routledge journals. Exhibitions as curator include *Uneasy Spaces*, an exhibition of work by 19 British-based artists working in photography and photo-video (New York, Sept - Nov. 2006) and *Facing East, Contemporary Landscape Photography from Baltic Areas* (UK tour 2004 - 2007). Her book, *Land Matters: Landscape Photography, Culture and Identity,* is due publication 2010. Other publications on landscape include Liz Wells, Kate Newton and Catherine Fehily, *Shifting Horizons, Women's Landscape Photography Now*, 2000. She is Professor in Photographic Culture, Faculty of Arts, University of Plymouth, and convenes the Land/Water and the Visual Arts research group.